THE PALM BEACH EFFECT *Reflections on Michael Hofmann*

D1313032

Arturo Di Stefano, *Michael Hofmann* (2012)

For an account of the painting, see page 204.

The Palm Beach Effect

Reflections on Michael Hofmann

EDITED BY
André Naffis-Sahely & Julian Stannard

First published in 2013
by CB editions
146 Percy Road London W12 9QL
www.cbeditions.com

Prefaces, bibliography and compilation
© André Naffis-Sahely and Julian Stannard, 2013
Copyright in individual contributions remains the property
of their authors

The rights of André Naffis-Sahely and Julian Stannard
to be identified as editors of this work have been asserted in
accordance with the Copyright, Designs and Patents Act, 1988

Printed in England by Imprint Digital, Exeter EX5 5HY

ISBN 978−0−9573266−0−6

Contents

Preface

JULIAN STANNARD

In 1984 I fetched up in Genoa. I had been living in Milan for several weeks, in the apartment of Francesco Alberoni. I realised he was a writer (the author of *Falling in Love*, a columnist for the *Corriere della Sera*) only when I wandered into Feltrinelli's and saw an enormous picture of him, his latest book piled up beside it like panettone. One day I took a train to Genoa and got a job at the Faculty of Foreign Literature. I left my one decent pair of shoes in Milan. I had enough money for a second-hand typewriter. I explained to my Iranian flatmate that I was going to write poems. He handed me a crate of pistachios. With nothing but yearning, and removed from any poetic hub, apart from the city which had its own poetic of dilapidation, I sometimes treated myself to a *TLS*. It would have been there, I guess, I came across Michael Hofmann.

During the summer vacation I was for a while back in London. I went to Hatchards: '*Nights in the Iron Hotel*. Do you have it?' The assistant, not much older than myself, seemed happy. 'We don't right now but' – *sotto voce* – 'I have the book at home. I'll photocopy it for you. Do you have an address?'

Having lived in Piazza della Posta Vecchia for six months I had as yet received nothing through the Italian post. The bookseller's proposal, therefore, seemed kindly but fanciful. Sometime in 1985, however, an envelope arrived from Hatchards – photocopies, most of them legible. I walked up the marble stairs in a state of excitement. In a city of syringes, I had my first fix of Hofmann. In 1986, or 1987, I managed to buy a copy of *Acrimony* and by now the fix had become an addiction. At some stage, as Tony Williams says of himself in 'Hofmania', I must have 'learned "to manage" my condition'.

It is difficult to describe the power of that hit. Was there a singe of heat? There was an absolute knowingness, a risk-taking, an absence of flummery, an utter readability! By 1987 I had plundered the glass-cased shelves of absent professors, so my collection of poetry was almost respectable. I'd discovered the Genoese poet Giorgio Caproni – 'Quando mi sarò deciso / d'andarci, in paradiso / ci andrò, con l'ascensore / di Castelletto.' Here was a poet writing about the streets (named) I was walking down. As with Hofmann's London, here was a poetic terrain which was entirely convincing. Mark Ford argues that Hofmann's metropolitan poems are 'among the finest London poems of our era'.

I ought to add that, as an undergraduate, I had met Fleur Adcock at a university reading and was impressed by the fact that poems might sound (almost) like ordinary conversations. I sent her poems to which she was kind enough to reply, so here too was a poet who was part of my hit-and-miss education. Adcock-Hofmann-Caproni, a weird trinity perhaps. Not one of them English, though 'Englishness' has not infrequently been the focus of Adcock and Hofmann's writing. In any case, all of this was useful for an aspiring poet who'd turned his back on Thatcherland. You looked for writers who got under your skin and hoped for the best.

Genoa provided its own psychological geography. You didn't need a classroom, you could look at ruined buildings and walk down rat-infested streets, what Dickens had recognised in *Pictures from Italy* as 'the rapid passage from a street of stately edifices into a maze of the vilest squalor'. And, of course, one could escape to the coast, the Riviera of bougainvillea and oleander – exquisite, delectable, deathly. Everywhere, in fact, *la poesia*: Dino Campana, Camillo Sbarbaro, Eugenio Montale, not to mention Pound, Bunting *et al* and the poetic undertow of Shelley/Byron. Professor Bacigalupo hoisted his jib in the

Bay of Poets and conducted seminars off the fishing village of Zoagli.

In this improvised canon, Hofmann was by now centre stage. His poems from communist Europe, his London poems, his refusal to dance around the mulberry bush resonated with the somehow disinherited city in which I now lived. *Dépaysement* seemed a gift, and his ease with crossing frontiers, his ready employment of German, his suggestion that an 'English' poem might not be written entirely in the English language, was not, in effect, completely removed from the modernist programme, even if he was seeing it through the Lowellian prism of the lyric – solipsism through the back door, or more brazenly, through the door at the front! If the young Pound was all show and orange socks, Stephen Romer gives us a description of Hofmann at Cambridge as the mysterious loner 'with a black hat'. One imagines Hofmann, the dark prince, wearing a ruff, at the high table of poetry.

And the voice! A young man's voice without the prevarication of youth, gleefully lugubrious, irreverent, insouciant! I took it with me through the *vicoli* of the city; lines slipped into my head (and remain in my head): if I found myself walking fast I was walking fast 'to lose weight', not, mind you, that it ever seemed to work. I have a memory of reading Hofmann under a high ceiling whilst listening to Leonard Cohen: 'There's a concert hall in Vienna / where your mouth had a thousand reviews / There's a bar where the boys have stopped talking / They've been sentenced to death by the blues.'

The Palm Beach Effect was a necessity and we've been fortunate with our contributors – novelists, translators, editors, critics, academics, erstwhile students, friends of the poet, a gifted contemporary artist who has gifted us the cover image, and a platoon of poets. It felt especially gratifying that so many of Hofmann's contemporaries were eager to contribute: a cause for celebration,

Julian Stannard   ix

an acknowledgement of debt, a timely re-evaluation of a literary career spanning a quarter of a century. And gratifying too that the quality of argument should, again and again, illuminate and entertain. C. K. Williams admires the drive of Hofmann's critical writing, arguing that poets all too often put up with a level of commentary that is lame and wide of the mark. In these pages a community of poets from across the world has provided the critical and creative engagement Hofmann deserves.

And there's no lack of variety – essayistic enquiry, anecdote, reflection, observation, material from interview. The book transcends the tedium of pedestrian scholarship but will provide, *inter alia*, a lively document for future readers of Hofmann's work. Poets (one thinks, for example, of James Lasdun or Stephen Romer) who were sometimes the 'addressees' of Hofmann poems or were part of the occasion of the poem write from their perspectives; we follow the progression of the fledgling (if assured) Cambridge poet in the early 1980s to the greatly admired poet-critic-translator of the twenty-first century. And, thanks to former students at the University of Florida, we are given fascinating accounts of Hofmann the teacher. Now that we live in a world of workshops (is there no end to it?) it's gratifying to see how Hofmann can turn the occasion into an assault on platitude and bullshit. And poets have, thankfully, provided poems too; the gathering is distinguished and includes, among others, Christopher Reid, Sarah Maguire, Frederick Seidel, Durs Grünbein, Hugo Williams, Michael Schmidt, Andrew Motion, Robin Robertson, George Szirtes, Alan Jenkins and Hans Magnus Enzensberger.

Although the focus of this project has been the writing of Michael Hofmann, with more than one commentator referring to the *sine qua non* of Hofmann's poetic signature, it's worth for a moment considering the wider context. Jamie McKendrick compares Hofmann's resolute use of the 'lyric I' with the neo-modernist principles of J. H. Prynne's 'Cambridge School', which was in the ascendancy when the poet was at Cambridge. His refusal 'to abandon a lyric tradition', in effect, might tempt us to position Hofmann (not, I suspect, that he would wish to be positioned) among the fractious tribes of post-war Anglo-American poetry. In simplistic terms Hofmann's lyric impulse seems antithetical to modernist 'impersonality' which scatters its legacies far and wide and sees its most exacting (and sometimes sterile) manifestation in L=A=N=G=U=A=G=E poetry. Romer maintains that Hofmann has been central in establishing the anecdotal – anathema in some quarters – 'as a mode, perhaps *the* mode, of *fin de siècle* mainstream British poetry'. Hofmann's poetic cuts across, gainsays and confirms certain orthodoxies. His embrace of the author of *Life Studies* inevitably recalls Alvarez's co-opting of Lowell *et al* for his 'turbo-charged' *The New Poetry* (1962), which lambasted the pusillanimity of English Movement poetry (the 'gentility principle') yet which nevertheless represented several of the poets who had appeared in Robert Conquest's offending anthology *New Lines* (1956). And Hofmann's literary interests often take us to a European modernist landscape, and are at times drawn to what Iain Sinclair celebrated in *Conductors of Chaos* (1996) as the 'remote, alienated [and] fractured'. Poets this side of the Atlantic wishing to escape the condition of Little Englandism have typically looked to America; the question of their looking and the poets they seek out become emblematic – San Francisco? Black Mountain? New York? Hofmann's engagement with Lowell, Berryman, Weldon Kees, James Schuyler, Frank O'Hara suggests contiguous traditions rather than an all-conquering single tradition. And, within a 'British' context, it's useful that Romer should cite Paul Muldoon (a poet whom Hofmann applauds in *Behind the Lines*). If the Irishman is all 'linguistic euphoria', Hofmann is quasi-therapeutic by providing 'a handle on our own helplessness, our fecklessness and unease'.

I wanted to stay clear of the term Festschrift because it

suggested to me we were giving out a kind of Lifetime Achievement Award. It's true that Hofmann is now older than '[His] Father at Fifty', an age which might have several of us recognising the 'bleak anal pleats' appearing under our eyes. Yet, notwithstanding the development of his poetry in *Corona, Corona* (1993) and *Approximately Nowhere* (1999), I can't entirely separate the Hofmann of today from my memories of reading Hofmann in the 1980s, almost (if not exactly) a Rimbaudian experience that left a lingering appetite. The poet has translated prose voraciously but the volume of poems has not threatened to breach the levee. It is revealing, perhaps, that 'Broken Nights' (*Selected Poems*) should have Hofmann 'Groping for a piss', hence rubbing shoulders, as it were, with the Larkin of 'Sad Steps'. This *pas de deux* with the English curmudgeon might hint at poetic withdrawal, the subtle pleasures of parsimony; after all, the delight of a truffle lies, in part, in its rarity. Yet the poet has not yet reached a venerable age, and nor has he departed for the Horn of Africa. Hofmann's readers remain, as ever, in a state of anticipation.

Preface: Under Different Flags

ANDRÉ NAFFIS-SAHELY

It's easy to see why Rustam is the most popular character in the *Shahnameh*: when still only a boy he slays an elephant with a single blow before going on to spear the obligatory dragon and lasso evil demons like cattle. While Rustam performs only seven labours, unlike his colleague Hercules, even his horse is hard as nails, once even tearing a lion apart with his teeth to protect his master. Yet rather than the Persian Hercules, Rustam is the Persian Achilles. Both are near-invincible; both spent time in exile during their youth, seducing royal princesses and fathering sons they unceremoniously leave behind. Sons that are destined to follow their fathers into battle; yet while Neoptolemus fought alongside Achilles on the beaches of Troy, Rustam and Sohrab were to meet as champions of their respective armies, under different flags. Both men are determined to win: Rustam to protect his reputation, while Sohrab wants word of his exploits to reach his father's ears, whom he thinks is altogether elsewhere. After all, Sohrab has never seen Rustam and doesn't know the real identity of the man he's about to fight. The two champions wrestle, and just when it seems Sohrab is gaining the upper hand, Rustam stabs him in the heart. By the time Rustam realises his mistake, Sohrab has died in his arms.

Anyone fascinated by Michael Hofmann's poetry would be well served by watching *My Father's House*, which was aired on the BBC in November 1990. The documentary pits father against son, Gert Hofmann the novelist versus Michael Hofmann the poet. Here too we see father and son under different flags – as Michael was later to put it in 2008, 'it was as if we had divided the world between us; my father got prose in

German and I got poetry in English'. The documentary opens with Michael reading the closing lines of 'Fine Adjustments' from *Acrimony*:

> It was a fugitive childhood. Aged four, I was chased
> round and round the table by my father, who fell
> and broke his arm he was going to raise against me.

We then hear Michael describe his anger at being left at boarding school in England, when after years at British and American universities, his father decided to return to Germany 'in order to live closer to his language'. This is another story where the quest, in this case the father's literary ambitions, triumphs over the son, who is left in the margins. At least Telemachus got to stay at home! The first time we actually *see* Michael in the documentary, he is wearing the black coat and fedora ensemble described in James Lasdun and Stephen Romer's essays at the beginning of this book. As he reads out his poems to an audience of Eton boys, the gawky, pasty teenagers stare in disbelief. When the floor is opened to questions, a student asks: 'Were you worried that your relationship with your parents might be affected by your writing poetry about them?' Michael hesitates and then replies, 'I think I was probably being a bit naïve . . . I thought the fact that my father was a writer would protect me from a non-literary response, but it didn't happen. It was better, more honest, maybe even more German to come to them with my concern and criticisms.' 'Criticisms' is one way to put it. There's no mistaking that the younger Hofmann is on a war footing: three minutes into the documentary we see a close-up of him in a barber's chair as his curly locks fall to the floor, as if he were one of the GIs in Kubrick's *Full Metal Jacket*. All his life has been leading up to this point – to the catharsis of *Acrimony*, to the peregrination of the truth-telling child poet as he wages an emotional war with an often elusive father. The anger is palpable, but so is the affection, as well as the curiosity. Sohrab dies in Rustam's arms because father and son don't know each other. In a way, Michael's poems about his own father were an attempt to get to know him; as he himself put it in one of his letters to Michael Schmidt just before *Acrimony* was published, Michael intended the poems as 'footnotes to his [father's] life and work', as if he were a scholar documenting an unsolved mystery.

What the documentary adds to the poems is that it provides a portrait of the emotional turmoil that is caused by the literature, but also what prompted such fury in the first place; Michael's last words in the documentary are: 'if you have the power to hurt someone, I suppose it means they still love you, or something like that, and I wanted to be assured of that.' Yet outside of the personal dimension, Michael's poems are themselves a superb documentary: they capture the smouldering sparks as fathers and sons debate the great questions of life. Through them, we see sons as they really are: volcanic, inappropriate, inspiring awkwardness and embarrassment in their fathers – fathers who despite it all tend to accord their sons a modicum of respect. After all, sons have every reason to feel aggrieved: they have not lived long enough to lose their ability to be outraged by the world, outrage that is often the only true engine for change: a chemical reaction that sees sons 'buzz' round their fathers 'like an electron', as Michael writes in *Approximately Nowhere*'s 'Last Walk'.

I started reading long before I learned how to live; which is why I still turn to books first. Of late, I find myself re-reading early favourites, the great *Bildungsromane*, mostly either German or Russian: books like Goethe's *Wilhelm Meister*, Novalis's *Ofterdingen* and Goncharov's *Oblomov*, surely the greatest anti-*Bildungsroman* ever put to paper. Unfortunately, *Bildungsromane* are often erroneously billed as coming-of-age stories, whereas they usually have more to do with disillusionment; the best of them gyrate around the most pressing question of our time: can individuals truly fulfil themselves while simultaneously remaining part of an increasingly complex society? Most German writers I've read don't seem to think so. It is no coincidence that Günter Eich – whom Michael has translated extensively – concludes his poem 'Dreams' with the following: 'Be as sand, not oil in the thirsty machinery of the world!' This – earnest, foolish, essential! – obsession with peeking inside the machine is something at which modern German literature has excelled, thanks to the clear-eyed intensity with which it has denounced the widening chasm between individuals and society, that process of alienation whereby we become simple cogs. If we agree with Heiner Müller that *Germania* is where 'spear' (*ger*-) meets 'mania', 'a form of insanity characterized by great excitement, with or without delusions, and in its acute stage by extreme violence', then literature too, just like politics, is war by other means. This is a challenge Hofmann clearly accepts. In his poetry, people are often bleached, unhappy ghosts floating around the perpetually morphing, jagged metropolis; and since nearly all his poems are episodes from his life – and he has tended to publish them fairly chronologically – I think his work will stand as the finest *Bildungsroman* in verse written during the closing decades of the twentieth century: a poem on an epic scale, whose narrative stands out for its lapidary quality.

It is cause for hope in a truly cosmopolitan world to see so German a poet express himself so effortlessly (and inventively) in the Anglo-American idiom and carve out a crucial place for these questions in the world of English-language poetry. The German wunderkind as an English poet. It can't have been easy; wunderkinds usually have more to worry about than late-starters. Their work doesn't tend to age well: while young, their boyish charm aids them when in a tight spot. Old men, like Thersites, who point their accusatory finger are usually mocked and rebuffed. It seems we prefer our underdogs young.

★

A few words on the book: this is not a Festschrift; Michael has many years still ahead of him and is far from the point where, to borrow from Richard Wilbur, writers become the good, grey guardians of art; secondly, Festschrifts are sometimes rife with encomia, whereas I see *The Palm Beach Effect* as a space where Michael's friends, peers and admirers – new and old alike – congregate in critical tribute. As C. K. Williams, another of our contributors, put it in his book on Whitman, 'all great poems, by their very definition, by the way they colonise and amplify and enhance the music of our own inner voices [. . .] ask us to be greater than we are, and if we read them well, even show us how to begin.' Michael Hofmann's poems have rented spacious suites in my mind, and even if I wanted to, I doubt I could ever evict them.

Londoners

JAMES LASDUN

In the early 80s I was employed as one of half a dozen in-house readers at Jonathan Cape, in their old Bedford Square offices. We were all writers and it seemed to be understood that we would spend as much time keeping up with our literary pals as we did reading manuscripts. Poets and novelists would drop in for coffee, or we'd spend hours nattering with them on the phone. Magazine editors would come sniffing around for our latest discoveries. It was like a club within a club, complete with comfy chairs and stacks of periodicals; a last redoubt of gentle-manliness in a profession that hadn't yet, quite, caught up with the rest of the world.

It was Hugo Williams, part of this cosy cabal for a period, who introduced me to Michael Hofmann's poems, which had just begun appearing in the *TLS*. I have to admit I felt stricken by them. I could see at once that they were amazingly good, but also that they were good in ways that were going to have a calamitous effect on all my assumptions about poetry. I'd dismissed the possibility that one could achieve the kind of high-intensity experiences I was looking for in a poem by any other than the most elaborately wrought verbal means. To read these coolly stated, deceptively prose-like poems with their implicit disavowal of anything calculated or orchestrated, their apparent disdain for extended argument or metaphor, and yet feel the same ferocity of emotional and intellectual impact as I found in Yeats and Lowell and Plath, was a disconcerting revelation. It also didn't escape me that this approach opened the poems to aspects of contemporary life – pop, politics, all the dreck and clutter of daily urban existence – that my own methods (such as they were) simply couldn't accommodate, and naturally this added to the general sense of being undone. The *coup de grâce* was that, for all their avoidance of conventional poetic effect, they were ravishingly beautiful pieces of writing; exploding with caustic wit, phosphorescent description, jags of plangent eroticism, and those squalls of weirdly joyous verbal music the like of which, to my knowledge, no one has produced before or since.

Hugo and I and Xandra Hardie – now Xandra Bingley – convinced our bosses at Cape that we should sign Michael up and we invited him in to the office. Not surprisingly it turned out Faber were also interested, and it was gloomily understood that he would go there if they made an offer. They did and he went, but it took them a few weeks to come to the decision and by that time our rooms had become a regular port of call on Michael's London peregrinations, and he and I had struck up a friendship.

As with the poems so, at first, with their maker. What initially appealed to me – an unformed, murkily embattled twenty-three-year-old – was his diametric unlikeness to myself; his benign self-possession, global perspective, and air of having long ago figured out what did and did not need to be read, watched, listened to. Everything he thought, interested me, and I was still pliable enough in my own views to learn new things and – thank god – unlearn some old ones. I can still hear myself trotting out some remark about poetry being a *craft*, only to be met with a pained furrowing of the brows and pursing of the lips and realizing the utter inadequacy and banality of this position. For a short time I tried imitating his poems – an embarrassing memory comes to me of something full of pre-emptively resigned lust and knowingly disillusioned politics, all peppered with German and Latin and set in a Tube station – but even when I'd realized the futility of this, I continued (and still continue) to find echoes of his highly distinctive tone, syntax, cadences, stylistic tics, in my own prose and poetry. Specific images too, I realize, looking back. Where could the tampon 'like a dipstick' in my poem 'Buying a Dress' have possibly come from if not the 'spark-plugs mixing with tampons' in Michael's 'Touring Company'? My appropriations stopped short of the black fedora he wore and the Balkan Sobranies he used to smoke, but a good chunk of his personal canon quickly became incorporated into mine: *Under the Volcano*, *Buddenbrooks*, Musil, Schuyler, Bishop, Iranian movies . . .

I'm not sure what Michael got from me in return. I probably knew more about food than he did, or cared more, though he's the only thin person I know who can out-eat me, and I've grown fond of his buttery cooking. In terms of literature I think I put him on to Brodsky; later I suppose Ovid. I couldn't persuade him to read Auden properly or Burroughs at all, but I remember him being impressed by the presence of Brecht's poems on my bookshelf, which he took to be the sign of a more cosmopolitan outlook than most English poets had. I don't know if it really was that, but it raises one of the large things we did have in common, which was our uncertain relationship to our own Englishness; complicated by Jewishness on my side and Germanness on his. It wasn't something we talked about at that time but we both surely felt it, and felt drawn to each other because of it.

We also had in common high-achieving, high-visibility fathers; again not something we talked about much, but it deepened the understanding between us, along with the sense of being a little oddly positioned *vis à vis* our own achievements. I suspect it bequeathed us each a bit of an *aut Caesar aut nihil* complex (there, some Latin), which has no doubt caused both of us difficulties at times, but which I like to think we've somewhat overcome, with a little help from each other.

I've been trying to remember those first years of our friendship. Of course I have the singular luxury of needing only to open those first books of Michael's to bring them back: precise details as well as the general atmosphere. We ate long lunches at the Tramontana as per 'Fidelity'. We went for epic walks around grotty 80s London as per 'Nighthawks'. In Kensal Rise Cemetery we rejoiced to see a gravestone with the name of a poet on it who'd dissed us both. We introduced each other to our mates and sometimes got together en masse – at Stephen and Bridget Romer's house in Senlis, or Geoff Dyer's squat in Brixton, or the Eric Gill/David Jones monastery in Capel-y-ffyn that Robin Robertson organized every summer for a while.

We're neither of us great talkers; when we did talk it was more about politics than literature, and possibly more about clothes than politics. Not much about girls (as Hugo once ruefully joked, 'he doesn't talk dirty', but then nor do I). When we disagreed about something factual we'd settle it with a bet. In Mexico Michael declared with sublime intransigence that the Mason Dixon line ran along the Canadian border, and that the flocks of obvious (if rather small) pigeons in Cuernavaca were in fact quail. These rare but striking lapses from omniscience put me in mind of Sherlock Holmes's apparent ignorance of the fact that the earth revolves around the sun. The lacunae become, somehow, further evidence of the genius. And I suspect I am not the only friend of Michael's who feels a little ploddingly Watson-like in his company, or, for that matter, who regards him as something like the Sherlock Holmes of British poetry: preternaturally attuned to reality, somewhat inclined to disappear, and always several leagues ahead of everyone else.

Early Days

ANDREW MOTION

Those first stabs at friendship hurt at home
given such *peinlichkeit*. It only went to show . . .

Better the pub, then, where silence mattered less.
My mother. Your father. Departures and arrivals

(as in: lives and reputations). England growing
richer and heavier, like the grimy charity lifeboat

re-launching now and again under the weight
of a little loose change. What did you do all day

I wanted to know. That was the right question
if your keen 'Mmm-mmm' was anything to go by.

Metaphor(s) for England:
Michael Hofmann's *Nights in the Iron Hotel*

FRED D'AGUIAR

In an *Independent on Sunday* interview on 25 May 2008, Michael Hofmann said, 'I think a big part of my writing poems at all is to make myself English; and that means not being straightforward.' That a poem could further the poet's apprenticeship to English-ness struck me as poetic gold when applied to a revisit of my appreciation of Michael's first published collection, *Nights in the Iron Hotel*. Through the 1980s I read the book (and heard most of the poems on many occasions). I took the German location of the poems and the European sensibility implied by an immer-sion in the language and culture of Germany and its environs as largely autobiographical in nature. I assumed that Michael's first book was the traditional *Bildungsroman* with an added twist of metropolitan cool seen in the book's well-wrought irony and in the bold autopsies performed on the sexual excursions in many of the poems.

The forty poems of *Nights in the Iron Hotel* begin with 'Here's Looking at You (Caroline)', which echoes Humphrey Bogart's playful line to Lauren Bacall in *Casablanca*, 'Here's looking at you, kid', a toast and a come-on. Additionally, the title nods in the direction of that Yeatsian gaze – the cold evaluative eye – to check if that vision still has currency for helping a poet in an emotional quandary. The temperature of that look is the trouble-some property of the degrees of warmth (read sentiment) and cool (read distance) relative to the subject under study. Looking isn't simply a position contemporary British poetry modulates to varying degrees on a sliding scale of emotion and its lack. Look-ing is obedient (and disobedient) to strictures outlined in the 70s by John Berger in his seminal text *Ways of Seeing*. The Caroline in parenthesis in the first poem is the addressee, the poem's second person pronoun, 'you', offered as direct address to an absent person and planted there to counter the reader–reflex to insert himself into the poem as the intended subject. The look is a relatively new approach to the love poem advanced by an inordinately young and talented poet – he's just twenty-three! – full of savvy and evasion, simultaneously up close and personal in its scrutiny and able to muster an artist's design of studied removal from his subject.

The simile in the first sentence stretched over almost two lines emits a calculated shock of intrigue retained to this day, 'Having your photograph on my bedside table/ is like having a propeller there . . .' What? How? Why? The three-dot ellipsis (almost a drum roll) leaves the reader time to catch breath, regroup and plunge ahead, impelled by the narrative promise to see just how the photo and propeller relate to each other and how the author intends to convince the reader of the veracity of his proposition. Both photograph and propeller share a condition of stasis but with a function of verve written into their definitions: as a living active body and person in the photo and as an object for motion commonly associated with propellers. The middle section of the poem with its talk about history projects and the visual aids that go with them is the 'how' part of the poem: it establishes the idea of flight and the emotional condition of separation from the loved one. Flight and the adventurist spirit always acting in deference to a personal motivating loved one present an opportunity for the poem's speaker to understand the nature of his love and longing for the Caroline in the photograph. A project about aviation becomes a love poem about the affects of absence on the heart. The places and their distances from the location of the speaker are listed – 'Nürnberg 100; Würzburg / (home of the Volkswagen) 200; Berlin 500' – and serve as reminders of the distance between the speaker and the person named in the poem, distance in this instance being emotional as well as spatial (he is literally nowhere familiar). The educational projects have clear parameters but the subject of the poem, by contrast, remains de-limited and inscrutable, and apparently beyond the reach of the usual research methods. Nevertheless, a study of the photo is helped by comparing Caroline with an object removed from its usual environment (that lonely propeller) but the act of looking at her and coming to terms with the history of the relationship is tantamount to embarking on a journey fraught with danger. The final two lines stand out as reminders of the affection that underpins the enterprise of the poem's witty conceit: 'The pioneers of aviation were never alone – / they named their machines after their loved ones.' Saying to a lover that s/he resembles a propeller may seem like a non-starter as far as pick-up lines go and just plain wrong for being so seemingly counter-intuitive, but in the hands of the adventurer-poet the trick of making the link and proving the opposite to be true becomes the formal success of the poem and the poem's massive achievement, its 'why'. It rings true as well for the process employed by the poet: he marshals everything at his disposal to cope with his feeling for Caroline.

The next poem in the book, titled 'Dependents', touches on all of the above relations of removal from a loved one and involuntary contemplation about it through a study of ordinary and apparently unrelated things in the speaker's immediate surroundings. It opens with an introductory first stanza about the poet missing his lover as he regrets postponing her visit. An incidental television programme about prisoners in a prison camp sets him off on a meditation about the prisoners' lives without their lovers. The apparent asymmetry between physical incarceration with the various vigorous attempts to connect with people outside the prison and the mental anguish of the free speaker in the poem incarcerated in his emotions and unable to act become symmetrical. The two sorts of isolation – one physical, the other emotional – bear comparison but not before

Michael, the poet, points it out. I enjoyed the cultural anthropology of the poem, its excursions into the quotidian as ways to explore the numinous. The efforts of those prisoners may be foiled for being too obvious, but at least theirs is an effort of some sort and they are not caught up in the permafrost of emotional catatonia. The poem's reversal takes place over the heady dash of five quatrains: the free become seen as trapped while the imprisoned make heroic gestures to gain freedom.

The thematic concern of just how much can fit into the tight space of four lines with their endless stream of implication of imagery spills over into 'Diablerie'. Most of the intrigue of this brief sketch resides in the relationships between the double locations of the speaker. Is the speaker addressed or engaged in an instance of self-regard? If there is an addressee, the 'your' subject of the poem, and an outside speaker (the poem's 'absent-presence' – I borrow this term from Toni Morrison's *Playing in the Dark*, her study of blacks in classic American literature), then the relationship of 'someone else's child' to the speaker becomes a matter of some intrigue. It could be a case that the child belongs to someone else and is a stranger to the pair, speaker and addressee, or more to my taste for corrupting and complicating reality, that the child really is someone's else, and not the speaker's child, so the reader is forced to think about how that child alters the relationship between the speaker and the person holding the child. The coded nature of the poem – stubbornly private and so eminently porous in its vulnerability to rampant interpretation – may be its most-winning aspect. There is a hint of Martian imagery in the image of the girl-child as a crab in a devil's 'red romper suit'. What comes across too is the speaker's great distance from the child – there is none of the usual parental or even humanist empathy of fuzzy warmth for small helpless humanity to help bridge the hostile gap. Instead the gap is defined by the distanced perspective, the sheer cool, alienated and detached regard for a threat, tinged with jealousy (if we see that child as a go-between). This all sounds overly contingent but hints at the deep textures of Michael's imagery.

'Day in the Netherlands' embraces the subject-inclusive and plural pronoun, 'we', in order to explore the subtle drama of a disintegrating relationship. The poem's tone straddles private and public spheres. Sounding as if locked in private discussion between a speaker and a silent listener, the tone is amplified through the megaphone of a city tour, a formal device that advertises the poem as public property, as something designed to be overheard. The couple is displaced and so up for scrutiny. The speaker for the pair sets up a binary between the confinement of the city and the confines of the relationship. A small prison built into a bridge ('Amsterdam's thinnest house') mirrors the poem's final image of 'My room opened off yours, / it could have been a cupboard'. Separate rooms denote distance between the couple but the 'cupboard' dimensions of the speaker's room suggest something stifling akin to the city's 'prison-cells built into the supports of a bridge'. Think back to the poem 'Dependents' with those prisoners dreaming of the outside world as one image locked in with that of the free poet imprisoned in his isolation and the symmetry between two apparently unrelated things becomes clear under the poet's meditative eye.

That eye has a tendency to roam from one topic to another but in 'Touring Company' the arena of personal relationships gets a second treatment. The first approach to the personal made by the previous poem, 'Day in the Netherlands', suggested a foreign place and hideaway space, those nether regions of the body (desire) and emotions (possibly love). In 'Touring Company', the heartbreak third line, 'it feels sick to be alone again', could not have been more direct in its declaration of the poem's theme and the poetic procedure for its diagnosis and treatment. Isolation finds its objective correlative in the 'Nautilus' imagery of splendid isolation coupled with a vacuum seal. The idealized perfection of the Nautilus, positioned outside of real time, in a time of fantasy, contrasts with the dust and detritus of the speaker's loneliness: one is laboratory controlled, the other contaminated by the nervy and almost dirty realism of a 'charlady'. Both realms, imagined *and* real (rather than Lowell's split of 'something imagined, not real'), find mediation via an outlook that seeks a middle ground between them. In twelve lines of the first stanza, the poet's tightrope narrative must balance engagement with messy reality counter-weighted by a clinical approach to it.

The second stanza serves as back-story to the first, by going back in time to one day earlier than the time of the first stanza, in order to reconstruct the life of the absent partner, a busy actor locked in playing small parts in *Macbeth* that necessitate multiple and repeated bloody deaths. It is startling to see how the blood and gore of her acting life – so much dying here as opposed to the utter lack of coitus, that small death, between the couple in the first sanitized stanza – 'invites' the vitality of blood 'into our private life' but only in terms of seeping life away from the relationship. The actor, 'my biker', rides solo out of the poet's life. Clearly the speaker wishes he could ride pillion! She vanishes from his life but forgets her 'vanishing cream', her make-up cleaner, so she may have to remain messy off-stage with her on-stage make-up, one reality bleeding into the next. Her practical engagement with reality and the imagined life of the actor double up in the poem's image of 'spark-plugs mixing with tampons in your handbag!' Those plugs cannot ever be emblems of desire but their proximity to tampons, the lifeblood (rather than the *Macbeth* blood of melodrama), goes some way to planting the seed of it in the reader's mind, inviting a reader to link the two. Flipping the order of the stanzas, so that Nautilus follows blood, reveals some of the tension between the poem's form and its overflowing content that generates so much of the poem's electricity.

The formal dexterity grappling with a poet's messy reality

finds its best outlet in 'First Night' with its third line, 'You move the fifty-seven muscles it takes to smile', which denotes just how the poet's lens, his clinical way of seeing, defines reality. Poetry never works by numbers but must be felt (the 'communicates' portion proving so much more important than the 'understood' other half of Eliot's equation). The precise count of the muscles as a formal device emits a charge of recognition for the reader that is diametrically opposed to its lack in the person who performs the action of smiling. 'Plato's great longing' for symmetry between art and love finds a home in this poem, though the speaker senses another poetic failure in keeping with Plato's conclusion that art is impossible because love is improbable.

The speaker of 'Miracles of Science' tries to come to terms with being cuckolded and finds it hard to do so without the help of science, hence the 'miracles' of the title. In this instance the miracle offers little respite in that the best the hurt victim can hope for is 'In seven years, after the cellular renewal of my body, / I will be a different person.' Well, yes, time heals, but memory survives that biological transformation and the irony of the statement is that the precise hope for a lessening of pain matches its hopelessly romantic conception steeped in science. The second miracle is the poem's containment of both scientific enquiry and romantic ideal. The drama in the monologue turns out to be the speaker's abject inability to know what is being said for that insight is available only to the listener.

On what turns out to be a rare occasion, the poem 'A Feminist Ballet' begins with a thesis, a signpost pointing to the subject of the poem, its about-ness. 'The colour in life is supplied by women . . .' That by-now familiar use of multiple full stops as ellipsis, the what-how-why comprehension gap for the reader, does not mean that the speaker of the poem believes this statement to be the case, but that it is worth the procedure of a poem to weigh the pros and cons of it. The poem's two big gestures, first on the literary history front 'Thomas Mann's

Aschenbach' followed by 'the captains of German industry', test whether life's colour really is owed to women, or whether men wield an equally worthy palette. The feminism of the title rests in how much ironic separation and real daylight exist between the woman in the 'baggy workman's overalls' on the one hand, and Aschenbach and those captains of German industry on the other. Not so much, it turns out. The industrial types delude themselves and parse the world in terms of unhelpful binaries, 'Like anarchists, they see things in black & red.' That outlook is as faulty as the yearning by Gustav Aschenbach in Mann's *Death in Venice* for 'an unimpeachable Absolute'. Both desires turn out to be useless acts against the inevitability of death. The person best outfitted for life appears to be the woman in those overalls, 'the colours of the rainbow: Roy G Biv'.

That palette, largely emotional, becomes simplified when applied to sex, as in the poem, 'Museum Piece'. The poem begins in a setting that might pass for a strip club: 'The room smells of semen.' But after its first three lines and characteristic ellipsis, the museum setting of 'erotic prints' is established. The proper subject of the poem is voyeurism. The 'we might be watching ourselves' remains ever watchful of social behavior refracted through a poet's lens: art imitating life as much as life imitating art. 'Museum Piece' pairs nicely with 'Mannequin', as the latter continues to explore the vicinity of social and sexual mores. High art and sex-shop objects jostle in the first four-line stanza followed by a complete stanza in parentheses, which invites comparison and contrast with the first stanza. A final line wants us to see the relationship between an appreciation of high art and a need for sex objects as two comparable versions of desire with similar kinds of voyeuristic reflexes.

This neat symmetry is really put to the test in the next poem, 'Entropy (The Late Show)'. By now the telltale pairings that are held up for interrogation to yield insight about each other should be a kind of home for the reader. The questions of what, how, and why lose some of their shock-quotient but none of their need for finding newer and more telling versions of truths. The 'split screen' of the TV harks back to early cinema with tricks that shocked an audience new to the moving image but deployed here as commonplace. The turn of the poem and its breakage and repair occur after the colon and line space at the end of line ten. Line eleven's indented opening 'game of darts' completes an enjambment of a sentence that begins on line eight, and the reader is meant to be surprised and amused. The dexterity takes off from this point of the poem. The 'entropy' of the title hinges on how the darts players try for bull's eye. Some of what the poet may wish for the poem belongs to that hit-and-miss technique of playing darts.

There is a European tourist aspect to the first collection and a fitting preoccupation with the meanings of a German heritage for a poet thinking in English about the meaning and extent of his Englishness. The family poems portray the usual dysfunctional family members held together by the inscrutable glue of a bloodline and, at the same time, punished by that sense of the filial. I wonder how much of a model Michael Hamburger served for Michael Hofmann since the father/son nexus figures so largely in *Nights in the Iron Hotel* and in the second collection, *Acrimony*. The flourishes of metaphor in many of the poems may be indebted to the Martian poetry of Craig Raine, Christopher Reid and others. But Michael is light in his use of it to help a poem make its emotional appeal. And perhaps to avoid being showy at the expense of the central concern of the poem so that show becomes the only victory of the poem, Michael quickly turns down the volume of bravura in his poems for a quieter, 'come-hither' invite to the reader.

The poem 'Family Holidays', one of the most outwardly autobiographical in the book, positions the poet as an outsider in a family of mother, father and two sisters. Each person stays in a private zone in a stultifying atmosphere of mutual dependence dramatized by the final two lines of the poem, '. . . Every day I swam further out of my depth, / but always, miserably, crawled back to safety'. The crawl of the swim is an act of desperation as well. The repeated attempts to get away from the family enclave carry their own dangers until it dawns on the poet that no matter how far he pushes the boundaries of escape there is that inevitable return and therefore no way for him to escape that familial bond. If ever there was a case made for Larkin's childhood as a 'forgotten boredom' this is it, with a dollop of the sinister thrown in for good measure.

Each poem presents a separate occasion, but thematic relationships abound between clusters of poems. The title poem, 'Nights in the Iron Hotel', belongs to the relationships category (though it spills into existential hubris as well). It is the best poem of the book and the one with most elements associated with a Michael Hofmann poem. The gap of the couple's hotel beds 'at a hospital distance' suggests the sanitary and the insane, the isolated and the badly in need of sustenance. On a hopeful note, or what stands for a hopeful gesture by the speaker of the poem, those separate beds signal trouble and harm between the two but not an end to the impulse to repair things, seen in 'I push them together'. In a poem that is only eighteen lines long and set in Prague, with the couple away from home and so forced to be together in an awkward and fragile relationship, the couple has a lot of work to do and much emotional ground to cover if they are to make it. The old 'iron curtain' of their location separates one from the other. In the middle of much malaise the urgent need for action is belied by an impulse in the speaker to depict his surroundings in such a way that it overcomes the implied death of the relationship. The final image of 'a gymnast swings like a hooked fish' underwrites agility and captivity simultaneously. Even if the two are doomed, the imagination escapes thanks to its accurate rendition of an emotional dilemma. Salvation cannot ever inhabit the poem but circles it as an act of reading. The actors in the poem are lost but the audience for it leaves renewed by the experience, the drama of the poem.

The phrase 'metaphors for England' is Michael's, from his interview with Fran Brearton in *Thumbscrew* (No. 13, Spring/Summer 1999, pages 30–46). I threw in the parentheses in my title to draw attention to the ambitious reach of the book as a project on Englishness rather than simply incremental stabs at the idea, and in deference to Michael's masterful deployment of parentheses in his work that draws attention to those Frostian roads not taken, alternative routes, suggestive alternatives and abiding influences on the poem's outcome. I threw in a colon as well because Michael privileges nouns and adjectives over verbs at a time when most poets who paid attention to the publication of Seamus Heaney's *North* in 1979 took to heart Heaney's covenant-like call for all practitioners to be quickened into 'verb, pure verb'. Basil Bunting helped this idea with his directive to poets to avoid adjectives because they 'bleed nouns'. For Michael to promote nouns meant going somewhat against that grain. It meant he had to put many other supporting features around nouns to make them the things they purport to be, while working against the idea of the poem as some self-conscious act. Not easy. The two – one for the poem, the other against any action in favour of making a poem, of forcing it – appear divergent, contradictory and irreconcilable. Those supporting features make all the difference. They include parentheses as a way to subtract from the notion of a main clause as the main subject of the poem and draw attention to the true subject as somehow hidden and in need of teasing out into the open. The main clause is the decoy for a larger claim on a more slippery topic captured fleetingly in parentheses. Or put differently, that main clause looks brighter by virtue of the aside; the contrast helps to make the case for one while introducing the other. Both add a perspective to a mood. The lesser clause usurps the dominance of the main clause by taking the attention of the reader away from what the poem began with and moving it into something tangential to it. As such the poem emulates thinking with its quantum leaps and approximates to the quality of life experience as inherently imagined and recalled. If thinking and experience appear amenable to the various forms of poetry in Michael's work the obverse is true as well: that thinking and experience present themselves as governors of form in his work. It is as if Lowell's something imagined were reconciled at last with his something recalled.

A Black Hat, Silence and Bombshells

STEPHEN ROMER

The black hat and the black coat I was familiar with, before I knew their owner. It was Cambridge, the beginning of the Michaelmas Term, 1976. My second year, I was half way up Castle Street, in the dampest digs in town. I recall a kind of fug over everything, from the rank stairwell to my second-floor room. Cooking, laundry and gas. To employ a Hofmannesque tripartite construction. And damp. Our heavy landlady would toil up and down the stairs, with a child in tow. We were a huddled group of exiles from college, all of us reading English, though not in any way strenuously. It was Victorian Novel term, and my second-hand copies of *Little Dorrit* and *Middlemarch* lay unopened on the table, where they began to grow verdigris. It was more important at that time to be considered a thespian, which was apparently what 'the beautiful people' did, and most of them were 'reading English'. A part in a play at the ADC, and above all, to be seen in the mirrors of the ADC bar, that was the glamorous thing. And to meet budding actresses. I was no good at it, though. So the other thing was to gather in a friend's room, slump to Dylan – these were the years of his great revival (or one of them), *Blood on the Tracks, Desire, Street Legal* – and smoke. One of our group rolled joints studiously, sitting up at a desk, and it looked uncannily as though he were writing an essay. So 'writing an essay' became code for rolling a joint. It was not done, in those far-off days, to be seen working (though it turned out some of us had been, traitorously and furtively). And it must have been in the rare studious moments at my table, in those damp digs in Castle Street, that I first glimpsed the figure in black, apparently surveying the town from the top of Castle Hill.

If I had known my Balzac, I might have thought – there is Rastignac, when he climbs to the top of Montmartre and cries out his challenge to Paris, the city he intends to conquer: *A nous deux maintenant!* As it was, having in my first year read medieval drama, I thought this was a symbolic figure, placed there as the scourge to my idleness and lust. I spoke excitedly of the fitful apparition in the black hat to my friends. They were inclined to disbelieve me. From what I later understood, it seems my vision of Rastignac was the more accurate, for the figure in black turned out to be a fresher at Magdalene, hence the proximity of Castle Hill. It was also rumoured that there had been some scandal in the interviews for English at Clare, and that an interviewee had spent a night in protest, sitting under Clare bridge. I did not then connect the two figures, if they are to be connected. Under the bridge, or on top of the hill, whoever it was clearly had a gift for the theatrical gesture, and also for getting unusual perspectives on a place.

I cannot exactly remember my first – real and not ghostly – meeting with Michael Hofmann; but I consulted a mutual friend, the art-historian James Malpas, a polymath who back then would alternate Strauss's Tone Poems with tracks from The Clash, and kept an assiduously detailed journal. James tells me the meeting was at a party in 'a resplendent Clare Gardens, due to the recent floods' in June 1978, my last year, when I was back in college. James had already spoken with some awe of the poet in the year above him, a figure who excited intense speculation, a loner who wore a black hat, and whose sparsely furnished room sported an enormous poster of James Joyce, also in a black hat. By that time, I was implausibly half in charge of the University poetry society: we hosted the visit of a frail, seraphic David Gascoyne, barely emerged from a long period of alienation, the altogether more robust and drunken visit of George Barker, who made my girlfriend cry by suggesting she give up Chinese and have babies, and even a youthful Andrew Motion came down from Hull, to read to us. I don't remember Michael attending any of these meetings, and certainly not the weekly workshop, a sometimes untender forum where some of us cut our teeth. And it was not until we had met a few times that – I recall this vividly: on the turn into Trinity Street by the Round Church – I was recounting the story of the figure in black, when Michael confided in his soft-spoken, dulcet tones that the figure in question must have been himself.

It is difficult and delicate to write about a friend and contemporary, still in the prime of life and in rude health! – who has become – this volume proves it – a considerable literary figure, and one that has influenced many of us. Still, since I have accepted the challenge I must hope for the subject's indulgence, and the reader's, if I strike the personal note – for I cannot honestly write about MH, especially in those early years, with the dry impersonality of the critic, as though – to quote from *Acrimony* – 'half my life had never happened'. We were close. There are poems in the first part of *Acrimony* which recount shared experiences. I see no reason to conceal this. Michael stayed with us in France – in 'The Realm of the Senses' he observes how 'The yellow Citroën sits up and fills its lungs' – this was my battered old Lemon that became a rusting eyesore in the pretty medieval town north of Paris where we lived. In 'Epithalamion', a persona speaks, or a voice, which recounts a wedding in which, 'ladies hats outnumbered our friends', and improvises freely on an anecdote I later told about my own honeymoon – the Fawlty Towers-like set-up where the owners were obsessed by their dying dog in the drawing room – and (I could add) there were the geese that met us on arrival and tapped censoriously at the car door. Michael came to our wedding in 1982, and I received his poem a few months after with some bemusement. It is important to record this and not skate over it, for a part of friendship with the man, initially, was about 'getting to know the ropes', which were never conventional, and to many baffling. Usual modes of behaviour or response did not apply. The event (my wedding) is quite recognizable in the poem, the voice that speaks the poem belongs to the bridegroom – that is, the poet adopts my own voice to 'speak the poem'. I did not demur when Michael showed me the poem – it was already in galley form, presumably accepted for publication. And therefore I have no cavil with this. It became clear that this use of personal/autobiographical material in his poems, often involving others, recognizably friends or lovers or relatives, was a part of his poetics from early on, indeed *the personal* – being personal, as much as getting personal – is a credo of his work (as it was, famously, of Lowell's) – and either one accepts this or one does not, either one goes along with it, or one does not. This needs saying. It is a question that every poet (and every reader) must decide for him or her self. Early on, perhaps unconsciously, but later quite consciously, Michael declared war on the 'expected thing', especially in a place as socially hidebound as England. He could drop a bombshell, very quietly. In retrospect I now see the poem has actually refocused my own vision of the occasion – and his apprehension of our, or at least of my, unease was correct. But it is of huge importance to me (I wonder if he recognizes how much?) that he should have said, on presenting my wife and I with the poem, words to the effect, 'I hope you'll accept this as a token of solidarity.' I did so then, on trust, and I do now – re-reading the poem it is the sympathy – the empathy – for our plight, caught up and somehow stranded in the 'social mill' – that comes through clearly. It is also very funny. It was startling, sometimes disturbing, often engaging, and always riveting to relive shared experience through the filter of a Hofmann poem.

But his early poems did just that – they were startling, disarming, shocking, disobliging, funny, and above all sophisticated. They were low-key and off-key, and they were knowing. They gave off a tang, like a violent dose of salts. They had European smartness and range, unavailable then to most of us, and they were politically savvy. They were also intimidatingly modern. *Il faut être absolument moderne* is as axiomatic for Hofmann as it was for Rimbaud. It is a memorable moment in my own literary life, when I found – it must have been mid-June 1978 – a bundle of poems, half-tucked under the bed in my college room on which he had been sitting, left there by Michael for me to find, after he visited me for tea. I cannot exactly say (I wish I could!) that I 'discovered' Michael Hofmann; for one thing I didn't have the clout – as Craig Raine or Hugo Williams did and were to do later on – to announce him 'to the world' by publishing him, but I must have responded quickly, and with the greatest possible encouragement. Michael may correct me, but I am pretty certain I was among the very first to read the earliest poems. I don't need to have them by me, the phrases remain – 'the fridge bellowed like a young tractor'; 'there was a new régime: we had curried dragon for breakfast'; 'the snake-headed street-lamps'; 'I rode my bicycle very slowly round the block, once'. This last line, if I am correct, was the end of a poem called 'Solemn Young Poem'. It struck me even then that MH was a league ahead of the rest of us; while we were writing solemn young poems, he was writing a poem *entitled* 'Solemn Young Poem'. He was streets ahead in his controlled irony. The poems we offered up to the workshop had all the usual faults of youth – they were over (or under) literary, they were showy or they were awkward, they were not sufficiently formed, or seen 'in the round'. Hofmann's seemed to spring into being fully formed. He was a phenomenon, an *énergumène* as the French say.

In an interview he gave some years later, Michael recalled his Cambridge years, and he mentioned knowing Peter Robinson and myself, and commented 'but there was no sense of common purpose', and in that he was right. How could there be? I at least could not fathom where these poems of his – and in those days they had a Surrealist, or perhaps even an Expressionist tinge to them – came from. I had emerged from reading Yeats entire, an experience which shook me to the core, but also started me on a dangerous, hieratic, metaphoric process which involved the idealization of experience, the 'vision of reality', the impermeable artefact, the golden bird of Byzantium. I was inspired in particular by his translation of Maud Gonne into a being with almost legendary attributes – 'was there another Troy for her to burn?' etc. All that grandiloquent, high-falutin muse-poetry stuff. Nothing could provide a greater contrast than Hofmann's confessions of unease, aphasia, disenchantment, in his minute, porous and culturally up-to-the-minute descriptions of London, Cambridge or Munich, his local dystopias. He found his material so much closer to hand, in the lovingly listed attributes of his own 'damp lung of a room', or in the habits of his co-tenants in the rambling house in Chaucer Road, Cambridge (my tuppence worth of annotation to 'Between Bed and Wastepaper Basket'). The increasingly personal – say, rather, the overtly autobiographical – content which seeps into *Nights in the Iron Hotel* and reaches its high point in *Acrimony* also left many of us, including myself, bemused, admiring, gob-smacked, dazzled and to an extent uneasy.

How this early, fully-formed poetry came into being was for the moment a mystery, and Michael certainly wasn't telling. Perhaps I was not asking, or daring to ask, either. I never sought to intrude like that, and nor did he. Discretion reigned. There were unspoken, mutually accepted 'no-go' areas in our conversations. Of his personal presence and charisma, and of (let it be said) his great good looks under the black hat, one could dilate at length, though he would hate it. But everyone who met him experienced, underwent, overrode, shared or suffered his silence. Michael in those days was intensely silent. Some took it for arrogance, others for shyness. Certainly he could 'out-silence' anyone I knew. An anecdote recounts the dry comment of one of his Cambridge tutors, who remarked when MH reappeared at a supervision after several weeks of unexplained absence, 'Ah, Michael, there you are, we have missed your pregnant silences . . .'. I believe he was not unduly troubled by remaining silent, and yet it was in my experience an 'attentive' or even 'expectant' silence, and he was glad when it was broken, or a subject was broached that he could enjoin. It was most painful in moments of one's own dismay – when his silence was not required, but comforting speech rather, and this he could not easily offer – but there again one apprehended an acute 'fellow-feeling', even if it remained unvoiced. For his experience of unhappiness, of unease, of general difficulty ('we are fascinated by our inability to function') we need only turn to the poems. And there too we may find traces that explain this habit of silence. A study could be made of modes of silence in Hofmann's work – not silence in any grand Steinerian sense, related to the 'unsayable' – but the physical constriction, the 'shroud of earnestness and misgiving' as he himself puts it in 'Night Hawks', the poem dedicated to James Lasdun. In *Acrimony* we find the condition included in the poem 'Impotence':

> Most evenings, I was aphasic, incapable of speech;
> worn down by tolerance and inclusion. [. . .]

In the word-perfect poem 'Friction' we find a couple suffering:

> Our silence is irksome and confrontational,
> As you sit across from me, I could wish you away:
>
> turning the pages of a book, your pen grinding
> on my paper – I quarrel with each manifestation.

More significantly perhaps, is the review of his childhood, especially in relation to the looming figure of his father Gert

Hofmann (who is key to understanding so much of the poet's personal drama):

> (My own part of the conversation: thin, witty, inaudible,
> as though I'd spoken in asides for twenty-five years.)
>
> ('Author, Author')

Or how any attempt at conversation on the part of the young child was literally drowned out by the continual noise of the father's radio:

> I kept up a constant rearguard action, jibing,
> commenting, sermonizing. 'Why did God give me a
> voice,'
> I asked, 'if you always keep the radio on?'

I note that the same poem ('Fine Adjustments') contains an almost prophetic reference to Joseph Roth – 'Once before, I left some lines of Joseph Roth / bleeding on your desk' – recruiting Roth as an ally in this filial confrontation with the father is obviously fraught with promise.

The speech of the father disparages, either by its bluntness or its boorish ineptitude, and the longed-for 'consummation' – a moment of genuine inclusion, as of men talking equal to equal – is endlessly deferred and frustrated. Either that, or it is the pointed tolerance and attempt to include him made by his adoptive family in England that reduces him to aphasia and exasperation. Despite his humorous treatment of it, no one should underestimate the culture shock Michael felt when as a boy he was 'jettisoned' (as he puts it in 'The Machine That Cried') in England to be educated. Much of the observational bite and humour of his poetry comes from 'having an edge', or being at a slight angle to his adoptive country, which was then very much England, even if he gravitates more towards Germany and the US these days. For myself, and I think it was the same for many of his contemporaries, it was not until the publication of *Acrimony* in 1986 that the full nature of Michael's overtly Oedipal drama was made plain – or indeed that the existence of his father, the celebrated German novelist Gert Hofmann, a master of irony, black humour, and controlled hysteria, capable of writing scenes of great cruelty and honesty, was brought home to us. The difficult relationship, the love-hate that characterizes it – underpinned by a fierce loyalty – was made even clearer by the strange BBC documentary in which Michael travelled out to Munich with a camera crew to interview his father (and his mother) about Gert's writing and his past, in what came across as a very public 'settling of accounts'. There had been other famous sequences to fathers by near-contemporaries – Paul Muldoon and Hugo Williams, notably – not to mention the all-important example of Robert Lowell's more general family history in *Life Studies*, but nothing quite prepares for the honesty, passion, anger, dismay – and wit – of 'In My Father's House'. Once again, it was fully-formed poetry.

The name of Lowell has been broached, and his is of course the central influence on Hofmann's early poetry. Others will surely testify to this. I rarely met Michael without a copy of one or other of Lowell's volumes in his pocket or his knapsack – frequently I think the Lowell not just of *Life Studies* or *The Dolphin*, but also the ragged, baggy, all-inclusive fourteen-liners that make up *Notebook* (a book, incidentally, that is amply represented in the selection from Lowell he made for Faber's Poet-to-Poet series). One particular memory in relation to this: in his room in Chaucer Road in Cambridge, I once picked up a copy of Lowell's Faber *Selected* (the yellow one, I think, with the poet's portrait smiling genially out from behind a pair of crooked spectacles). Many of the poems Michael had annotated *line by line* with a tick or a cross – according to whether in his judgement the lines worked or they did not. I was forgetting, as I write this, that during the post-grad years in Cambridge in the early 80s Michael was in fact working on a PhD on Lowell, though it was never completed. In the end, as he wrote to me, he was 'half-pushed, and half crawled' out of the programme, and he left Cambridge to settle in with his girlfriend in West Hampstead. The other poet he introduced me to was John Berryman, in particular to the collection *Berryman's Sonnets*. Berryman also had a tortuous relationship with his father – though in his case the father was dead – through suicide or misadventure he was never absolutely certain – and the concealing of certain facts by his own mother aggravated the poet's own emotional instability considerably. I came late to realizing the extent of the American influence in Michael's early work – there was Lowell and Berryman, but also the colloquial, wry, inclusively low-key Frank O'Hara, and he spoke enthusiastically of Weldon Kees and James Schuyler.

Michael remained in Cambridge, and in 1978–79, just as our friendship was getting going, really, I went to the US. Our early friendship was oddly characterized by near-misses and failed meetings, 'by-passes and flyovers' as Michael once put it. I went to Lowell's old stamping ground Harvard, as it happens, where I was not happy, sensing a subliminal steeliness about the place, despite the cheery American *bonhomie*. I mention it because MH, significantly, was the only person, when I went home briefly at Christmas, to notice that something was amiss, though I took care to hide my true state of dismay. After that I moved to France, which turned out to be for the duration, but we still met frequently, in London, and when he came to stay with us in Paris – picnics and cigarettes on the roof in Montmartre – or in Senlis. Then he went to Germany, and after that to Florida, for at least a third of every year. There was a holiday in Scotland, and a slightly hair-raising trek in the Pyrenees with my sister. Meetings have become rare now, but they remain precious. Walks over Hampstead Heath, a particularly competitive game of Scrabble at Thanksgiving a few years ago, at the home of James Lasdun in the Catskills. Soon after I returned from Harvard, Michael's poetry started to be published – many will remember that startling full page in *Quarto*, and how it was followed up by his inclusion in Faber's *Poetry Introduction 5*. We looked on in awe, gob-smacked yet again.

Despite the hurt and the dismay recorded in *Acrimony*, it appears that Gert Hofmann bequeathed to his son three precious things: a feeling for the writerly career (see Michael's poem 'Old Firm' with its moving, vocative address, 'Father, the winter bird writes bird's nest soup [. . .]'); a rigorous work ethic; and a sense of certainty about his own literary judgement. Michael Hofmann could and can unleash the most devastating criticism if he takes against a writer – his dismissal of Douglas Dunn's *Elegies* comes to mind, or more recently of Craig Raine's 'Martian' device; there was a serious hatchet job on a Hungarian novelist which lingers in the memory, and more recently and conspicuously still, his dismantling of the life and work (and even of the suicide) of Stefan Zweig. These swingeing attacks can seem full of animus, and like his hero Joseph Roth he can get personal. He can be biased and partisan. He can be decidedly contrarian – viz. his famous dislike of W. G. Sebald, whom he dismisses as overly Gothic and 'sub-Thomas Bernhard' – an opinion he is proud to hold in the face of the almost universal approbation accorded to this writer. He is similarly forthright, and controversial, in his 'robust' approach to translating modern German poetry (Durs Grünbein, Gunter Eich, Gottfried Benn), which on occasion takes the Pound/Lowell position to an extreme. In the end, time alone will tell how this type of 'versioning' (that can work brilliantly, if the *tone* is just, and justified by the original) will weather. I predict that the best of Michael's versions will eventually form a part of the Hofmann poetic corpus, much as *Imitations* does of Robert Lowell's. Speaking of translation, we were involved, with Jamie McKendrick, in a kind of three-horse race – though an excruciatingly slow one – when we were charged by Faber in the late 90s to edit their *20th Century Poems* anthology series in French, German and Italian. It was perhaps our one acknowledged moment of 'common purpose'.

Michael Hofmann's poetry, as George Szirtes wrote, reviewing the *Selected*, is a poetry of the nerves, and that is right. It is a poetry of accumulated detail, selected by an antenna that serves a centripetal sensibility, an egotistical sublime that processes phenomena and inflects them by means of a strong subjective surge. I note that the lists and the lines get longer, and more inclusive of detail, in each succeeding volume. It is a poetry of surfaces, patient, content to explore, eschewing metaphor and the grand gesture, profoundly metonymic and 'horizontal' . . .
  Trying to come to grips with it, I once defined it as 'atheistic' in its evolution of similes and apparently arbitrary, ad-hoc analogies forged out of wildly dissimilar and apparently rebarbative matter. Hofmann is the master of entropy – frequently he observes situations or relationships or matter in decomposition – how 'All things tend towards the yellow of unlove' –

> the marigolds
> develop a stoop and grow bald, orange clowns,
> straw polls, their petals coming out in fistfuls . . .
> ('Cinders')

There is a law in narrative fiction which says that any given situation is either improving or deteriorating, and Hofmann places himself firmly on the side of the latter. But the verbal energy crackles, even as he does so.
  It is premature to attempt to reckon up Michael Hofmann's poetry, or predict exactly where and how it will stand in the future, but one can say that if Paul Muldoon enfranchized the

poets of our generation by his linguistic euphoria, his playfulness and his winning tone, Hofmann gave us something equally valuable, a handle on our own helplessness, our fecklessness and unease. (I find I am using the preterite, but there is every likelihood he will produce more poetry . . .) He has the audacity to speak squarely and clearly out of his own experience, though he refrains, unlike Larkin, from speaking for everyone, and he makes only sparing use of the first person plural. Like Larkin's, his poetry takes care – sometimes exasperatingly so – not to get above itself. His poems assume their solipsism unashamedly, indeed it is their salient feature. And by doing so, of course, we see ourselves in them. He helped us to grow up, and to use material that was so familiar and close to hand we scarcely noticed it. The distance he seemed to have, so early, on familial and relational issues that most of us would not have noticed – observing, for example, a little boy who has 'the exemplary energy of the late child' ('On the Margins') – is the kind of psychological insight that is usually the gift of the novelist. But the poet is still at the centre of the poem – 'Back here, I feel again spiritless, unhappy, the wrong age'. He has also been central in establishing the anecdotal as a mode, perhaps *the* mode, of *fin de siècle* mainstream British poetry.

When we would meet in the early days, whatever the circumstances or the weather, however unpromising the surroundings, Michael would always prefer to walk rather than to sit in a café or a pub. An aerial presence, he preferred to be on the move. Getting comfortable, or remaining comfortable, was never Hofmann's thing.

Joy Ride

ANDREW ELLIOTT

I am driving in the Chevy Belair the Hofmann family rode in
in Michael's 'Day of Reckoning', west across America.
The wind has made much of my hair and, now that the sun is
    setting,
I indicate to overtake a pickup stacked with flat-pack quatrains.

But as I pull away I note its right front tyre too rapidly unravel
and as it swerves to keep control the pickup spill its wayward
load. I note all this in my rearview mirror just as later
I will note the trailer park for which that load was, doubtless,
    bound

and so pull in beneath the only oblong window in which a light
    might indicate
a wife is waiting up. I knock and she shouts, *Who's out there?*
It's the question I have always been dreading. Damn her dark
    Honduran eyes!
I play it safe, I say I'm not sure. *It depends on who you are in there . . .*

I was lucky she didn't blow me away. She wasn't short of fire
    power.
The following morning I led her to believe that a period of
    mourning
was in order, then took what I could from her larder and
    continued
to drive across America. I assumed the experience would have
    hardened her.

The sun was behind me now. What a lovely car the Chevy
    Belair is!
Two cacti stood by the road ahead. One was tall and thin, the
other small and fat. I picked them up. They're in the back
    though
if they don't stop yakking soon it could be the trunk that
    awaits them.

I'm checking if I've got enough duct tape – yup – when in my
    rearview mirror
a dot of immense if not infinite density appears to be gaining
    upon me.
Not good, driving west in a stolen car, so I pull over. *Ladies*, I
    say,
you're a prickly pair but it's been a pleasure, and run away into the
    desert.

Acrimony: 'My Father's House'

TESSA HADLEY

Writing will never get to the bottom of this big old subject, or to its end: the son's contest with his father, the father's struggle with his son, the more or less violent transfer of authority passed down through the generations of men. Women are interested in it too, naturally enough. (The transfer of female authority between mother and daughter seems beside it an equivocal and hidden thing.) No matter what new patterns men learn (or we all learn), this gristle of paternity still seems to require chewing over fairly often - and seems always to mean more than just itself, seems to open onto huge vistas: historical-scale, even biological. In the wonderful poems he wrote in the 1980s about his father, Michael Hofmann steps almost with a shrug into the well-used space where so many writers have been before him. He doesn't so much shuck off all the ready-made apparatus of understanding – the Oedipus complex and the anxiety of influence and all that - as shuck it on, making no apology. ('You hear this fellow in the cellarage? . . . Well said, old mole!') It's all so obvious that it can only be a beginning.

The protests in *Acrimony*, poems written when Gert Hofmann was still alive, might look earnest - even peevish - at first glance: the son spills over onto the page the disgusts and resentments, the wounded amour propre, that he can't get expressed in his father's actual presence (the very existence of the poems in itself is evidence of the intimidation). The father's 'salami breath tyrannised the bedroom', he fills the primal place with his smell, male animal marking his territory ('Bärli'). The boy wants his father's attention and approval, doesn't want to belong 'in the back' with his mother and the girls ('Day of Reckoning'). He longs to drink slivovica and talk books with his father, to be initiated into the male world: 'Family was abasement / and obligation . . . The three steps to your door / were three steps to heaven' ('My Father's House Has Many Mansions'). But 'the indulgent patriarch' only smiles 'the absent smile of inattention . . .'. 'We are as the warts on your elbows, / scratched into submission, but always / recrudescent'; he turns his son (and the wife and the girls) down, turns the radio on, or up. Once even, when, unusually, he's 'acceded' to conversation, he puts on his 'black armband' and takes his blood pressure, 'as though in the presence of an unacceptable risk' ('The Means of Production').

But the lovely joke-picture of that last image (the sheer pedantry of the great man's self-importance, as if deigning to communicate with his family might be a threat to his health) is actually the right spirit of the poems; they aren't at all peevish, peevishness is their subject and not their mood. This is a bitter, rueful, knockabout comedy of a relationship, in which both characters play out, as people do, their exaggerated roles: the father's bullying triumphant beastliness, and the son's puniness and hurt inability not to care. The son's protests aren't any more securely the poem's perspective than the father's careless strength-to-hurt is: both positions are open to the same ironies. This isn't to say that the tyrannies don't feel real in the poems: they do. But the point of writing them isn't for the son's sufferings to be vindicated (Hofmann in *Behind the Lines* quotes Brodsky insisting that 'the poet is never, in the final analysis, a victim'). The point is to get the sufferings written down accurately. The pressure behind the expression is just the same as if the tyranny hadn't been real, as if the writer were making a story up. The justice being done isn't moralising, it's to the truth of the whole scene, its texture and contents.

Hofmann has said that his own early poems have 'the shape and texture of bricks' (marvellously, as opposed to the kind of poems which are 'swans carved in butter'). 'Bricks' seems just right for the density of this writing: its chunky solidities, its plain style, its freighting all its apprehensions with real stuff. These poem-rooms are crowded with furniture and people, they share some of the qualities of novelistic realism – including their clear referentiality and sequential connectedness. And that play between the businesses of prose and poetry is a tormenting extra twist in the relationship between this poet-son and novelist-father. Writing ought to be the weapon of the weak son, displacing the real-life power of the father; what a cruel joke, to find your father-subject seated there before you at the writing desk, already holding the pen (imagine that happening, for instance, to Kafka!). Of necessity, other people's words precede you when you begin to write; but how it turns the screw on the old rivalry to find the father-subject in situ, in his all too bodily actuality, occupying the supposed-to-be-singular place behind the words. The writer-son is cheated, before he even begins, out of his exclusivity. 'You gave me a copy of your second / with the dedication: Michael, / something else for you to read. / Your disparaging imperative / was too much resented for obedience . . .' And the novel writing becomes entangled, for the son-character in the poems, with all the rest of the holding off, the patriarchal offence. 'You were a late starter at fiction / but for ten years now, your family / has been kept at arm's length.' ('The Means of Production'.)

So it feels inevitable that the son should choose poetry, which isn't his father's prose. And of course his election of poetry is much more, in the end, than a matter of being edged out or boxed in; it becomes his right and inevitable mode – and becomes the relationship with his father's work. The story gets told through those poised incompletions, those holdings-off or holdings-in-suspension, which poems are good at and which prose, with its necessity of 'one thing after another', finds harder. The stop-start narrative of the series of poems becomes a way picked carefully, and without forcing, through the thickets of their rivalry; the layered accumulations of impressions don't have to be fixed together in conclusion. The precise, right capture of the father's presence becomes in itself a kind of homage, without the poetry's ever disavowing the fraught knot of the relationship or its psychic violence.

The short 'Catechism' summarizes in one poignantly comical moment:

> My father peers into the lit sitting room
> and says, 'Are you here?' . . . Yes, I am,
> in one of his cloudy white leather armchairs,
> with one foot not too disrespectfully on the table,
> reading Horváth's *Godless Youth*. Without another word,
> he goes out again, baffling and incommunicable,
> the invisible man, dampening any speculation.

It's the almost archetypally teenage experience – burningly present to yourself, you're overlooked by the adult as if you didn't exist. Under the magnification of teenage angst, the banality of the pointless question (why ask it, if he can see someone to ask?) becomes laden, metaphysical. Are you here? And it's the question the concerned father ought to be asking, seriously, of the heir on the brink of coming into his adult intelligence; the son burns to answer, he longs to unburden himself to his father of his here-ness. But we don't know whether he does actually answer; the 'yes' in the poem isn't in inverted commas like the father's question, it might be unspoken. And anyway it was always a pointless question – what, in the real moment, could be an appropriate response? Instead the poem embodies its 'yes': the son offers himself, his contents, his state of play, in answer to the father's seeming interrogation, which is both dreaded and desired. The son is here, he's in the living room, of course, seated as if he's usurping (caught like Prince Hal trying on the crown), in one of the armchairs that are his father's (white leather, redolent of the style of an era the son's already outgrowing), reading a book that belongs to his father's generation and informs the son about his father's world (it was published in 1938; Gert Hofmann was fourteen in 1945). The title *Godless Youth* sticks to the youth now, too, in his gesture of exquisitely calibrated not-quite-disrespect (though I think it was also accidental – the point of the gesture wasn't meant until the son found how it might have looked, if his father had looked at it): that one foot on the table like a sign, a promise of things to come.

But the ultimate gesture of the father's power isn't in his disapproval (which would give the son a kind of advantage, in time); it's in his not even listening for any answer, or giving any further word. 'Baffling and incommunicable', the poem says: not the 'uncommunicative' which logic suggests. The father is the conundrum which the poem can't get past, or finally express. Perspective in the last line doubles around sinuously; now it's the father and not the teenager who is 'the invisible man, dampening any speculation'. Possession of the powerful eye, casting its look over the room, has passed from the father to the son, throwing the loop of his poem over his parent, failing to catch him, but finding his own strength in choosing the right words to communicate the frustration, the stubborn negativity.

The mother is present everywhere in *Acrimony*; but always in the back seat of the car, or just offstage, or filling – but mutely – the companion-space beside the father which the son also aspires to fill: or she watches from a window 'my father and myself, out walking, our hands held / behind our backs in the way Goethe recommended' ('My Father's House Has Many Mansions'). She's the half-abandoned wife, too, when the father has affairs in Ljubljana – the affairs mostly interest the son, Oedipally enough, as a part of the sexual underpinning of his wrestling with his father (over the scimitar and shaving bowl in 'Vortex', the castrating Struwwelpeter scissors in 'The Means of Production' and so on). 'In your absence', the son says in one poem, 'it's up to me to be the man of the house' ('Errant'). Reading the opening lines of 'And the Teeth of the Children Are Set on Edge', the first of two poems where the mother breaks her silence, we are likely to mistake them to begin with; aren't they addressed to the father as usual? 'Already', the son complains, 'I've spent a half-life cornered, listening to you'. But actually we haven't heard anything at all from his mother, until now; and she's got so much to say – which her son isn't keen to hear. 'I can see you've been waiting for me, preparing yourself. / There are few preliminaries. The words have been / gathering inside you, now they are ready to come out.'

Poor mother; why does her lament set her son's teeth on edge? One suspects, because it sounds so like his own, the same piling up of circumstantial details that amount to accusations ('His hotel bills / are mountainous, there are telegram receipts, the lot. / One day he went to buy himself a coat, and came back / with two parcels . . .'), the same hunger for an accounting, the same anguished anticipation of non-response. Bent upon becoming a man, the son needs to close his ears to how womanish he sounds in his own hopeless love (as in 'The Machine That Cried', when as a boy he's mistaken for 'Madam' on the phone). But because the poet isn't, uncritically, the son, he includes the son's exclusion of his mother's voice. The poet takes her lament – which was disdained – inside his words, her words become his own, become part of the record. Hofmann didn't include these two mother-poems in his *Selected*, however, and perhaps the change of perspective doesn't altogether work. Does the lament feel too naked, as if irony can't adequately protect it, inside the shape of the son's quotation? In this black comedy of family life, the absence of the female half (mother and sisters) is perhaps in itself more eloquent than any effort to include them. The exclusion is like a helpless confession of male-centredness – could even feel like a courtesy, that the writer doesn't pretend to speak for them. (A novel couldn't manage their absence in the same way.)

Insofar as these poems draw the map of a mind-world, then

this one is – and self-consciously – a very masculine place, with the struggle between father and son, and the riddling foundations of male authority, at its heart. (Incidentally, in *Behind the Lines*, Michael Hofmann's 2001 collection of critical writings, there are essays about forty-nine male writers and three female ones: though it's embarrassing to have counted. And it may be that imbalance is built in, anyway, to the European literary culture for which he is a passionate and persuasive advocate.) Traditions of taste and judgement and style necessarily get expressed, between the generations of writers, as prohibitions: against kitsch and sentimentality, naturally, and sometimes also against the obvious and the ordinary, the too-yielding or too-hopeful or optimistic. And sometimes those discriminations are felt as 'male', as opposed to a female sweetness. Isn't this the austere training in sensibility, which the father-poems in *Acrimony* so superbly skewer? (No doubt there are parallels with traditions in the formation of masculinity through, say, soldiering – or through ideals of male honourable conduct, whether of the working-class or gentlemanly kind.) No soppy talk, no friendly initiation of the son into the father's world, no chumminess: just work. 'You never cleaned your teeth, but they were perfect anyway / from a diet of undercooked meat; you gnawed the bones; / anything sweet you considered frivolous' ('My Father at Fifty'). The poet was trained in skewering, of course, inside the very tradition which has become his subject here. No doubt the tradition helped produce the poems' characteristic bold solidity, their un-wistfulness, and their distinctive reticence - for all the plain talk.

The father's power can't last. 'Bärli' begins with exasperation at how loudly the father fills the place – his smell, his signature; then modulates into a chill intimation when he has his tonsils out and can only croak over the telephone: the poet shivers at 'the faint breeze / that blew through you and formed words'. In 'My Father at Fifty' the eater of undercooked meat, with his austere writing discipline, lives on to become middle-aged and less inspiring: 'Your male discriminations / – meat and work – have lost their edge. / Your teeth are filled, an omnivorous sign.' Fathers don't only block the way to the desired authority, they also send back pessimistic news from life inside it, which somewhat taint the pleasure of possession in advance. Studying his father's heart medicines and his whitening beard, the son intuits the future with mingled dread and – what? Cool realism, perhaps, learned at the source. The reader has to wait for release in the more tender second sequence of poems in *Approximately Nowhere*, written after Gert Hofmann's death; there's no resolution to the conflict in *Acrimony*. Resolution, anyway, sounds too much like something out of that sentimental store which good taste repudiates (in an essay from *Behind the Lines* about his father's novel *The Conquest*, the poet writes that 'Neither the world nor the consciousness can be said to have truly changed during the process of inquiry, or investigation').

There's no resolution, that is, save writing itself, which can scrutinize the tragi-comic drama and communicate it and even find it funny – in the father's own best bleak tradition. When the poet in 'Digital Recordings' picks up his father's pen, it's not been handed on in any heart-warming moment of parental benediction or abdication, nor even deliberately stolen: just 'taken in error' (a trick of sound suggests terror, perhaps, whitening the fingers?). It's characteristic that this moment of significant symbolic connection should come about at last almost inadvertently (it's not even the final, valedictory, word in the book). The poem finds its way meanwhile to a lovely culminating joke about the ink, in which protest (blood ought to be thicker) and affirmation (writing's better) simply can't be separated out.

> My fingers whiten as they bunch themselves
> to grip my father's pen. Silver and surgically thin,
> taken in error, its ink is thicker than blood.

Repetitions and Strange Adjacencies

JAMIE MCKENDRICK

The title of *Corona, Corona*, Michael Hofmann's third book of poems published in 1993, which sounds like a Mexican oath in a Western, is derived from the poem 'Hart Crane' and describes the American poet's histrionic habits of composition:

> A sufficiency of drink, the manic repetition
> of a mantric record – any record – and he typed.
> Corona, Corona, Victrola, and a Columbia loud needle.

A prickly mouthful of brand names from the Jazz Age and the 1920s economic boom. Giving their own 'manic repetition' ('record . . . record'), the two Coronas refer presumably, I almost said respectively, to a cigar and a famous make of typewriter. Another suspect might be the Mexican beer – considering Crane's long sojourn in Mexico and the last section of the book dedicated to that country. In what looks like an embarrassment of riches, his *Selected Poems* omits this poem (along with several others including 'Biology', 'Dyptich' and – most regrettably in my view – 'Shivery Stomp'), so the book title has a somewhat orphaned air as it now stands in the *Selected*'s index.

The book is echoic in its ideas, its shapes and its sounds. Another meaning of *corona* is 'crown' and indeed the word appears in his poem 'Kurt Schwitters in Lakeland':

> Kurt Schwitters's tombstone was hewn in straight lines,
> *klipp und klar*, in the shape of a hat, brim – crown.

That line's alliteration makes its own corona. Repetition on a temporal as well as a spatial level is very much the theme of 'Guanajuato Two Times', the whole poem organized around a repeated conditional tense:

> I could keep returning to the same few places
> till I turned blue; till I turned into
> José José
> on the sleeve of his new record album,
> 'What is Love?';
> wearing a pleasant frown and predistressed denims;
> reading the double-page spread ('The Trouble with José
>   José')

the poem begins, and goes on to explore pairings, doublings, ghostings, repetitions, and near repetitions of many kinds. Another example can be found in 'Shivery Stomp', a poem that traces 'a strange adjacency' to the novelist Malcolm Lowry:

> to have visited so many of your sites, Ripe and Rye,
> Cuernavaca and Cambridge, and by fifty-nine days,
> never to have done time – a term – together

Again the alliteration and the phonetic slippage of 'time' and 'term', with their shift from prison to school plays on the theme of identity and near identity. A later line from the poem describing the England Lowry 'fled and died in' – 'Brick and lichen, pruned willow, prunes and the WI' – makes an even more intricate play on sounds.

In Hofmann's first book, *Nights in the Iron Hotel*, there were already some remarkable 'lives of the artists' poems – on the Expressionists, on Kirchner – but it's really in *Corona, Corona* that he gives himself free rein to explore biography. Seven years after his intensely autobiographical second book *Acrimony*, which tracks the painful relationship with his own father, the novelist Gert Hofmann, it could be thought that in these poems biography is autobiography by other means – 'It surely isn't me, pushing thirty, taking a life a night . . .' as the question is not quite conclusively settled in the book's first poem, 'Lament for Crassus'. Most of the first section is devoted to poems on writers, artists, as well as the musician Marvin Gaye. Like the last, many of these seem to have had serious trouble with their father – Dadd kills his own dad, Gaye is killed by his – and so the book in a conscious and curious way projects filial conflict onto a wider screen. And yet the artists and writers whose lives Hofmann 'takes' are as often also taken as examples – Lowry, Schwitters, Beckmann are all tutelary spirits to whom the poems pay warm tribute, 'a strange adjacency'.

The book has, roughly speaking, a tripartite form – the first section biography, the second autobiography and the third travel writing – three literary genres which the poems both regard askance and reinvent. Amid a generally chilly reception – or so I remember it in the immediate (and continuing) enthusiasm of my own response – one of the few reviewers that responded appreciatively and intelligently to the book was the poet Mick Imlah in the *Independent*. Noting the 'phenomenally rich vocabulary', he also speaks of the way the poems exploit 'diseased lexical harmonies akin to rhyme'. This is certainly a quality that distinguishes the collection from Hofmann's previous work, which for the most part had fastidiously avoided conventional rhyme and metre; although his poems allowed for subtle word-play, they appeared largely indifferent to 'music' – any acoustic effects that might be considered adornment. Here poem after poem admits a complex play on sound, repetition and assonance, and their arguments sometimes seem to advance through phonetics.

My only reservation about Imlah's suggestive phrase is that 'diseased', though it perfectly fits his first example from

'Biology' – 'all pocked, opaque, Venetian, venereal', gives scant acknowledgement to the more vital and vigorous part sound plays in these poems. Even where the speaker has a defeated or lassitudinous air, these phonetic effects act as a kind of counter argument: language is alive with patternings and possibilities.

A short poem such as 'Pastorale' may offer an example of how and why this is the case:

> Where the cars razored past on the blue highway.
> I walked, unreasonably, *contre-sens*,
>
> the slewed census-taker on the green verge,
> noting a hedgehog's defensive needle-spill,
>
> the bullet-copper and bullet-steel of pheasants,
> henna ferns and a six-pack of Feminax,
>
> indecipherable cans and the cursive snout and tail
> of a flattened rat under the floribund ivy,
>
> the farmer's stockpiled hayrolls and his flocks,
> ancillary, bacillary blocks of anthrax.

'Pastorale', bearing a dedication to Beat Sterchi, the Swiss author of *The Cow* which Hofmann himself translated, is mordantly anti-pastoral, but arresting in its display of both colour and harmonics. From the first image of the cars that 'razored past', the poem bristles with militaristic terminology, and with a dark irony insistently presents the bucolic in terms of the martial – the hedgehog's 'defensive needle spill', the beautifully observed 'bullet-copper and bullet-steel' of the pheasant's plumage, the 'stockpiled hayrolls' and so on. It reaches a sinister finale with an alphabetic chiasmus, literally *abba*: 'ancillary, bacillary blocks of anthrax'. Anthrax rhymes jarringly with that 'six-pack of Feminax' – itself an unhappy collision of gender attributes (the brand-name being a now discontinued codeine-based drug for period pains). Even the word 'bacillary', from Latin 'baccus', meaning rod, has an aggressive air in contrast to 'ancillary', from Latin 'ancilla' for 'handmaiden' – though in this case perhaps a handmaiden of war. The sounds become buzzing and armoured. If for the first time in Hofmann's work an almost Keatsian richness arrives in the language, here it's to subversive or uncomfortable effect. While these poems bask in the release of acoustic energies, it would also be true to say that they subject a long English tradition of *melopeia* (Pound's term) to a kind of critique.

The 'slewed census taker' – as Hofmann introduces himself in the first lines – walking against the traffic flow 'unreasonably, *contre sens*' (where the English puns on the French) is a singular take on the figure of the *flâneur*, whom Baudelaire dubbed 'le botaniste de l'asphalte'. This urban figure is given a comic twist by being exiled to an unspecified stretch of the countryside. No wonder he's 'slewed', and yet he collects his data, mainly road-kill, with an extraordinary determined precision and a dazzling palette.

Although Walter Benjamin saw the demise of the *flâneur* in the age of consumerism, Hofmann finds in this figure a continuing point of leverage. Characteristically a stroller around the metropolis, the *flâneur* has an inbuilt radar – lost in the crowd, he (a 'he' it is in all historic accounts) never abandons a sharp, perceiving eye and a leisurely sense of his own apartness. What Hofmann adds to this traditional figure is a set of very particularized character traits – the perceiving 'I' is at odds, disaffected, marginal, stripped of any external authority or even of the vatic tone that we might associate with a prototype of the *flâneur* in Blake's 'London' ('I wandered through the chartered streets, / near where the chartered Thames doth flow . . .'), and yet the poet remains a witness, whose trustworthiness is earned, at least in part, by descriptive virtuosity. So while the tone of the poem chips away at any sense of stable authority, the performance on the level of language re-instates it.

Something in the compression and compounding of elements in that last line of Hofmann's recalls a similar effect in Blake's poem's ending, 'And blights with plagues the marriage hearse'. For all that the speaker plays ironically on his doom-predicting role, and the poem moves to its macabre end with exaggerated emphasis, there is a reality which the poem reveals – anthrax (*bacillus anthracis*), a bacterium that affects livestock and soil, was tested on the Scottish island of Gruinard which remained contaminated for almost fifty years and has indeed been stockpiled by various countries, although Britain in 1956 renounced its use. Even in the land of the lamb the tiger's claws are visible.

Polluted, menacing pastorals are a strong feature of this collection, perhaps most definitively in 'Dean Point'. The poem which follows 'Pastorale', 'On the Beach at Thorpeness', begins:

> I looked idly right for corpses in the underbrush,
> then left, to check that Sizewell was still there.
> The wind was from that quarter, northeasterly, a
>   seawind,
> B-wind, from that triune reliable fissile block.

Like '47° Latitude' which precedes 'Pastorale', making a kind of atomic and chemical triptych, this poem catches the jittery feel of the time after the Chernobyl disaster in April 1986, the sense of likely irreparable ecological damage, which has – or at least should have – re-awakened with the meltdown at Japan's Fukishima Daiichi nuclear reactor in 2011. If the opening plays on a jokey paranoia, there is – as in the tired old joke – a great deal to be paranoid about, so the comic persona, if persona is the right word, has history on his side, and the comedy is of a decidedly uneasy kind.

This opening splices a pedestrian's traffic code with a detective *noir*, and has the strolling subject again at his data-gathering. By surveying a stretch of beach he comes up against what used to be called 'the military-industrial complex', and arrives at the blunt Churchillian final line: 'Jaw jaw. War war'. Another repetition to recall *Corona, Corona*. Sizewell comprises three A and two B reactors, so I take the 'B-wind' (which otherwise refers to a film printing technique) to be a suggestion of the emissions from the Magnox block. The stanza's last line with its run of three adjectives linked by assonance, 'triune reliable fissile', picks up the preceding poem's 'ancillary, bacillary blocks of anthrax'.

In the third stanza, nature itself seems to be complicit, or entangled, in the nuclear threat:

> A set of three-point lion prints padded up the beach.
> The tideline was a ravel of seaweed and detritus,
> a red ragged square of John Bull plastic,
> a gull's feather lying down by a fishspine.

The writing is densely allusive – the first image may come from Elizabeth Bishop's 'The End of March', another walk-on-the-beach poem – 'a track of big dog-prints (so big / they were more like lion prints)' – and the last line, with a desolate wit, transforms Isaiah's vision of the Peaceable Kingdom into a marine landscape of *disjecta membra*. (Another reference to Isaiah [5: 29–30] is perhaps audible here: 'Their roaring shall be like a lion . . . And in that day they shall roar against them like the roaring of the sea'.) In the poem's penultimate stanza, the acoustics intensify:

> The North Sea was a yeasty, sudsy brown slop.
> My feet jingled on the sloping gravel,
> a crisp musical shingle. My tracks were oval holes
> like whole notes or snowshoes or Dover soles.

Another feature that Imlah's review praised was 'an imagination whose way of thinking in shapes often brings geometry to mind: not just in incidental diagrams . . . but in the materials and organisation of whole poems' – this has indeed been a quality of Hofmann's work from the outset, from, say, an early poem like 'Shapes of Things', and it is a gift that has evolved dramatically. Here, in the o-haunted sequence of images that lay down near identical tracks on the ear, as in the last stanza's description of the tide that 'advanced in blunt codshead curves', an auditory as well as a visual imagination of a rare kind can be seen.

The prominence of the first person in this opening, 'I looked idly right . . . / then left', is a frequent element in these poems: '. . . where I walked' – line 2 of 'Pastorale'; or 'I arrived on a warm day, early, a Sunday' (line 1 of 'The Day After'). See also from the Mexican section: 'I leaned round the corner in a Gold Rush town –'('Las Casas'); 'I walked on New Year's Eve from Trotsky's house' ('The Out-of-Power'). Then there are poems by contrast that open in sedentary or supine mode: 'Picture me / sitting between the flying buttresses of Cuernavaca Cathedral' ('Postcard from Cuernavaca') where the participles wittily contend. Or 'I eat alone in a room with a net' ('No Company but Fear'). Or in ''47° Latitude': 'I was lying out on the caesium lawn / on the ribs and ligatures of a split deckchair'. This poem comes round full circle, a kind of corona, to end:

> as thick as pebbles
> on the beach. I lay out on the caesium lawn.

The cunning enjambment allows the title of Nevil Shute's nuclear apocalypse 1957 novel *On the Beach* to appear stranded. (The film of the same title had already figured in Hofmann's 'Shapes of Things' – so a repetition of a repetition.)

Each of these openings ostentatiously place the speaker very much in the foreground, as if to rile an aesthetic espoused by the 'Cambridge School' poets in ascendance when Hofmann studied there, and for whom this use of the 'lyric I' was, and is, a kind of taboo, and a sure marker of intellectual backwardness untinged by Modernism: 'the empirical derivation of poetry from exclusively personal experience', as Andrew Crozier put it sternly. Maybe it's wrong to conscript Hofmann into a battle in which he has no stake and probably little interest, but the question remains as to why the first person pronoun is so prevalent, central and insistent. In all of the openings quoted above there is little doubt about the irony, sometimes bleak, sometimes caricatural, with which the first person pronoun is surrounded. The 'I' is certainly not an unmediated construction: for all its continuity, it has to be made up afresh for the peculiar purposes of each poem, but there are unmistakeable traits in common throughout his poetry. It is worth noting, further, that the very distinctly located and personalized 'I' of *Acrimony*, in which the first person pronoun is seeen *in primo piano*, is no longer a necessary convention for these poems, but still remains as steadfastly insistent.

As has often been noted there is no mistaking a Michael Hofmann poem: it just couldn't have been written by anyone else. For all that this hyper-distinctive 'I' might destabilize the convention, he refuses to abandon a lyric tradition that has characterized more than two thousand years of European poetry and can be found in lyric traditions elsewhere that go back much further. Try as we might, we do not see through others' eyes, and admitting the partiality of perspective is a kind of basic honesty rather than a tyranny of the self. Quirky as the 'I' is in Hofmann's poems, it seems to be an un-excludable given, a declared perspective – the avoidance of which would by no means guarantee any greater integrity or objectivity.

The performance is always on a high wire, and the risk of solipsism is always there. The poet's self-portrait at forty in 'XXXX', an appealing poem from *Approximately Nowhere* (1999), takes this risk to its limits. It begins 'I piss in bottles, / collect cigarette ash in the hollow of my hand . . .', and ends:

> I am quarrelsome, charming, lustful, inconsolable,
>   broken.
> I have the radio on as much as ever my father did,
> carrying it with me from room to room.
> I like its level talk.

After his father's death, this poignantly recalls a poem from *Acrimony*, 'My Father at Fifty': 'Wherever you are, there's a barrage of noise: / your difficult breathing, or the blaring radio'. Though even here, in what looks like an entirely recursive moment, there's the ghost of an echo, from Gérard de Nerval's 'El Desdichado':

> Je suis le Ténébreux, – le Veuf, – l'Inconsolé,
> Le Prince d'Aquitaine à la Tour abolie:
> Ma seule *Etoile* est morte, – et mon luth constellé
> Porte le *Soleil noir* de la *Mélancolie*.

The unconsoled speaker in Hofmann's poem *carries* a radio rather than a star-spangled lute but the implied Melancholia bears a history that is not 'merely' personal. It's a shade antiquarian to suggest that a poem which begins 'I piss in bottles' needs an arcane allusion as ballast, but what I'm suggesting is that the 'I' used in poems as challenging as these comes with a dense history, however fleet and insouciant the manner might seem.

In its repetitions of sound and shape, its plethora of echoes, ghostings, and pairings, however, *Corona, Corona* seems to me to have found the most satisfyingly complex way of exploring both identity and the world beyond the self – a world more inclusive than could easily be found in any other contemporary poet.

Psalm

FREDERICK SEIDEL

Today is Monday, and I am carbon free.
I don't mean carbon free, I mean sweet land of liberty.
I mean I'm reducing my carbon footprint
As I walk fast past the freezing flowering on Broadway,
The pear trees blowing off steam in white bloom
Despite a sudden cold front chilling the warmth.
I hear airplanes high-fiving and helicopters choppering.
Fire engines bellow and ambulances going through a light go woo woo.
It's an election year, and it's time to declare whom you're for.

I'm for a fine Airedale named Hobbes –
After the philosopher, the dog walker walking him explains –
And I'm for all the other animals I greet on the sidewalk.
Hobbes! I can tell you're a good boy!
Hobbes pauses and looks up at someone
He can tell understands him.
A seven-year-old I'd never met came over to me
At Grandparents Day at my grandson's school
In Brooklyn, and started talking to me as if I were his.

He said both his grandparents were dead.
But don't you have four?
He said his mother was in Paris.
He said his father was buried at sea.
He was Huck Finn, with a gap
Between his two front teeth and in his story, who like Hobbes
Seemed to know whom he was for.
The trees in the center strip of Broadway not yet in bloom
Stick up like antlers above the ones in flower.

There is no excuse for not voting next November
For the clouds or for the stars or the moon,
And last night there was even a bright planet
Next to the moon sliver when I came home drunk.
The pigeons are cooing and moaning and mating
To my disgust down here on earth this Monday.
Today is Monday, and in Florida and endlessly
An unarmed black kid seventeen years old has been shot dead
By a neighborhood watchman, a Latino gentleman.

Who will watch the watchmen?
A huge angel perched on top of a tree in the bright sunlight
Of the Broadway center strip doubles the height of the tree,
And of course looks extraordinary, what an extraordinary sight
On its hind legs like a dinosaur, a monster angel standing on a tree.
I try to imagine a huge winged white of light,
Unmistakably the product of another dimension.
I bend down to tie my shoelaces that have come undone.
I know I will have to look up eventually into your gun.

Hofmania

TONY WILLIAMS

I wonder if people remember where they were when Michael Hofmann first made them gurgle with delight. For me it was on the down escalator in Mothercare in Sheffield: I read 'Lament for Crassus', the opening poem of *Corona, Corona*, with a growing incredulous joy, then stood in the basement amongst the pushchairs and toothing rings, chuckling like Muttley. I had previously puzzled over, tried, slormed through (I won't say *read*) *Nights in the Iron Hotel*, getting the grim bit but not the humour. Perhaps it would have helped if I'd read at the time his comment that 'I hope my poems aren't dismal; I think they're hilarious.' I think it was the fourth stanza of 'Lament for Crassus' that unlocked things for me:

> Crassus, the pioneer of insuranburn,
> with his architect slaves and firefighter slaves,
> big in silver, big in real estate, big in personnel.

It's hard now to recall the vertigo induced by seeing a word like 'insuranburn' in a poem about a classical subject. That mock-epic, grinningly bathetic collision of tones and periods is now a familiar Hofmann trope (perhaps, in the end, *the* Hofmann trope), but that day in Mothercare it dazzled me for the first time. Suddenly I got the joke. By the time I'd got to the end of the poem, the casual and complicatingly unfunny brutality of 'whose head was severed a day later than his son's', I was a goner.

The section that opens *Corona, Corona*, which prompted my first feverish episode of Hofmania, is strangely untypical of his work, a collection of pen portraits of various mainly cultural figures: Max Beckmann, Kurt Schwitters, Hart Crane, Marvin Gaye, Richard Dadd. It contrasts markedly with the more or less confessional atmosphere of his other books. (Hofmann poems are generally about Hofmann's own life, though if you like we can squeamishly preserve the nicety that Hofmann the persona is different from Hofmann the man. I'd say that's too easy: the poems are *about* persona-building, so unless we want an infinite regression of masks, we have in the end to accept that poets write about themselves, even if they make some of it up.) All in all, *Corona, Corona* is Hofmann's oddest book – not just that set of portraits at the beginning, but, after a middle section in which normal service is more or less resumed, a strange final set of postcards from Mexico which feels part travel memoir, part poetry western, part obsessive fan's pursuit of Malcolm Lowry (see how I'm cheating by reading Hofmann's enthusiasms as a reader into his own work). The portraits and the Mexico poems are the one time when it feels like Hofmann is choosing a subject, turning his technique to bear on something. Elsewhere it's as if the poems are spontaneous reactions to the conditions of life, a kind of insanely sophisticated shrug of amusement-irritation. The remark that 'the poems assuage my need for them to exist', aside from hinting why Hofmann is a less prolific poet than we might like, supports the idea that most of his work is produced more or less compulsively; *Corona, Corona*, on the other hand, seems willed, a book that someone deliberated over.

If that sounds like a sly way of criticising, that's because it is: from a critical perspective I think it is certainly not his best book. There's even a case for it being his worst (*Nights in the Iron Hotel*: coherent and savage, the style fully formed but not yet fully utilized; *Acrimony*: his best, the best book of poetry of the 1980s; *Approximately Nowhere*: richer, warmer, authoritative). And yet – and this is one of the ways I self-diagnose my Hofmania – in spite of this critical judgement, of which I'm not in any doubt, I'm not sure *Corona, Corona* isn't my favourite Hofmann collection. If *Acrimony* is *Highway 61 Revisited*, then *Corona, Corona* is more like one of the bootleg series: minor, playful, hardly to be taken seriously. And in fact there is something about this dual judgement ('that's a better album, but I prefer this'), something faintly absurd and hierarchical and self-indulgent that makes me feel like a music fan.

Another symptom of Hofmania is, well, having Hofmann on the brain. It's eased for me now, thank goodness (enthusiasms have to ebb, or they become limitations), but for a while Hofmann was pretty much the only star in my firmament, and a kind of wilful, young-man's, derivative irony my only writing mode. As it turned out, there were a few things I still believed in, and in time I came to understand irony as a single colour rather than the whole palette. Maybe I wasn't cured, but learned to 'manage' my condition. The residual symptoms include a wonderful and sometimes perverse having-to-hand of this peculiarly mordant oeuvre. Hofmann speaks of having carried Tom Paulin's *A State of Justice* with him 'everywhere' – it isn't quite certain that he means literally, but he does talk of repeatedly renewing his library copy of Ian Hamilton's *40 Poems*, so he has previous. His own four flimsy Faber volumes (*Night in the Iron Hotel* clocks up only 42 pages of poems) spent a fair few years in my satchel – OK, it was a laptop bag, but I didn't have a laptop – but more significantly they persist in that great Platonic satchel, the mind: blooming with post-it notes, the yellowed pages, packed with italics and proper names; the austere covers, the garish red and blue of *Corona, Corona* with the death's-head sun and the pink of *Nights in the Iron Hotel* faded to peppermint green on the spine. (Not everyone likes Faber's design philosophy, but it does, through its complete indifference to giving the reader a leg up, help to accentuate what Shklovsky might have called the bookishness of the book.) The contents are like some unhealthy canon or *Oxford Dictionary of Sardonic Quotations*. When I see gymnastics on the telly I mutter to myself, 'dizzying social realism for the drunks'; when I hear 'Freebird' I think of American college students having sex. I can't read an elegy for a father without comparing it, always unfavourably, with 'I cried for my father's inevitable death'. The whole project of writing about one's father feels unnecessary, impossible, in the light of *Acrimony*. The 1980s in Britain exists most clearly and convincingly for me in the first half of *Acrimony* – actually a little more than half of the book isn't about Gert Hofmann at all, but sets the stage, as it were, for his entrance, by letting us know the world in which Hofmann junior feels so spectacularly not at home.

In fact 'setting the stage' undersells the work's wider public commitments. I never felt that Hofmann was as bound up in *himself* as his great early influence, Robert Lowell, was. *Acrimony*'s dysfunctional personal relationships take place in landscapes which are analogously dystopian; either stands for the other, and this may or may not be a matter of chance. At first sight it looks either like the pathetic fallacy writ large, or like a cynical appropriation of socio-political conditions to match the colour scheme of autobiography. But we must take seriously the idea that the two elements are really (in 'real' life, that is) both governed by historical conditions. The depiction of place and of personal circumstance registers wider cultural and political circumstance, so that apparently personal situations are shaped by public historical conditions. In 'Freebird', violence characterizes the cultural climate at national, local, personal and linguistic levels, and the juxtapositions of public and private and linguistic brutality show how transgressions in one sphere serve not only to reflect but also to enable those in another:

> I was cuntstruck and fat. My tight chinos
> came from a Second Avenue surplus store
> that had an RPG dangling from the ceiling.
> Grenada had been; the campus killings came later.

[. . .]
The frat boy overhead gave it to his sorority girl
    steamhammer-style.

Hofmann's visions of both place and person are provided by cultural sources, from 'Rupert Brooke Country' to the van playing 'Greensleeves' and the tower blocks named, in an 'elementary deception', after famous figures in English literature: 'Dickens House, / Blake Court, Austen House, thirteen-storey giants [*groan!*]'. Typically the real landscape is dystopian because it deviates from what such sources lead us to expect. Similarly the persona's failures and frustrations derive in part from life and art's inability to match up to each other. His descriptions order the world in terms of authors and characters, from Des Esseintes to Dostoyevsky to Tolstoy to Le Carré. Literature, Gert Hofmann's (and later Michael's) business, is also the means by which they (fail to) communicate, and which provides the son with material with which to 'engineer' his identity. Such engineering on the personal level is different only in degree from the facile appropriation of authors' names for road names.

The accumulation of materials, whether these are cultural allusions, linguistic fragments or literal objects, is the means by which Hofmann depicts his subjects. Several commentators have worried that the seemingly neutral handling of such material might come close to forming an endorsement of the Thatcherite Britain it depicts, or at least that the failure to present a more positive alternative represents a serious shortcoming. Hofmann asked of Gottfried Benn, 'Given a synoptic nihilism like this, where is there to go?' and his own low and diminishing output might speak more eloquently than any critical contortions about the answer. Nevertheless there's an ethical dimension to this problem which seems to me peculiar to English poetry. Benn himself kept writing throughout his life, and Hofmann has hardly been idle, as the vast body of translations attests. It may be that the European poet is less worried in the end by the imperative to provide a humane or value-positive vision than his English counterpart.

Certainly it is as a European poet that we need to understand Hofmann. Julian Stannard has described the poem 'Albion Market' as 'Bayswater . . . suddenly informed by Weimar'. This poem and others like it achieve an implicit moral and historical comparison between 80s Britain and 20s Berlin, not so much by explicit juxtaposition or allusion but by selective adoption of tone and technique. The pessimistic and purposeful irony; the accumulation of contemporary images and materials, often without comment and sometimes without much in the way of syntax; the gallows humour: all these features of Hofmann's work and other more specific ones are traceable in the German poetry of the early twentieth century. There are others too – Lowell's ellipses and multiple epithets, for instance – but these may be more readily familiar to an English-speaking reader, and less significant to the work's tenor. By drawing on the German Expressionists' technical means Hofmann brings a new historical perspective into English poetry's view of England. The symptoms of this mania can be serious . . . Perhaps I shouldn't be talking about a disease at all, but a gateway drug.

David Malcolm has pointed out that 'Malvern Road' 'is, in a real sense, only a list of things connected with a place – the street, the maisonette, the buildings, the stairs, the furniture, the businesses and a tree'; this method is repeated in several of Hofmann's poems which portray temporary homes: shared houses, bedsits, hotels. The link between place and personhood is repeatedly suggested: the personae are guests or tenants, and their living arrangements reflect or determine their wider identity. The speaker of 'A Brief Occupation' asserts, 'I was not myself. I was just anyone.' The occupants of bedsits cling to their rooms as to the vestiges of themselves: 'The house is breaking up, and still I'm hanging on here.' In 'Retrospect' the speaker returns to old ground but feels no nostalgia:

I remembered only the declivity
of St Andrew's Hill when I saw it again,
not the gloomy elderberry ravening in front of the house,
not even the address on Windsor Road,

an Edwardian nest of damp and peckish students.

By implication the lack of memory in the present is related to
a lack of identity in the past: the speaker can't remember having a home here because as an exile, a foreigner, he never *was*
at home. He spent his time worrying about 'the *Fremdenpolizei*
come to repatriate me. / I still worshipped a blue acute Anglia /
for the name and the brainy space in the back'. The poem ends
with a contrast between the alienated speaker and the blind man
'so very much at home there, he stopped at the gate / to crumble
his white stick into his pocket', serving both to underline the
speaker's disconnection and to offer a homeopathic quantity of
redress. Although the speaker clings to (revels in) his sophistication and self-awareness ('I climbed the street again, with
the carpetbagging / eyes of a yapping estate-agent'), they may
themselves be the barrier to his finding a home somewhere.

The poems' method of cataloguing objects and episodes is
mirrored, and indeed effected, by the way they assemble fragments of language. 'Rondure' rubs up against 'humpity', 'squinny' and 'bimble' against 'cryogenics'. The poems are laced with
other languages, odd registers and slangy constructions. Alan
Robinson argues that Hofmann's style offers 'a chain of discrete
remarks which seems to emanate from a disembodied voice
rather than a fully realised persona'. But this isn't quite my experience of reading. The voice is dissociated from place – it
cannot be located as at home anywhere, least of all in the places
it inhabits – but it is not disembodied. The shoring up of fragments does constitute a persona of sorts, a kind of ultra-educat-
ed exiled European (Hofmann refers to 'bourgeois gypsies'),

continually knitting together multifarious cultural sources to generate an identity for the time being. Although the ironically assumed masks which construct the persona do not add up to an 'authentic' personality, this deficiency itself represents the authentic experience of large numbers of displaced and migrant Europeans in the last century and in this increasingly mobile century. Moreover one of the effects of globalization seems to be the diminishment of given local identity and a more willed (and wilful) construction of the self through cultural sources.

Of course constructing an identity is just what writers (as opposed to their personae) do in developing a style grounded in their reading. This is where we come back to the drunken immersion in Hofmann's work which I suspect I share with many others. One feature of what David Wheatley calls Hofmann's 'magpie' style is the continual allusion, not just directly to other texts but also, as I have indicated, technically to the practices of writers outside the English tradition. Hofmann's poetry, like his translations, makes available writers who have been underrepresented in the English tradition; and it isn't just a matter of making available in the manner of someone dressing a shop window. The breezy manner of Hofmann's allusions serves as a rebuke to the writer who is not reading widely and internationally. The enthusiasm and lucidity of his critical prose, and the contiguity of his interests as a critic and translator with his practical influences, encouraged me when discovering his work to see the work as an educational whole, as if not just the translations and the criticism but also the creative practice were designed primarily to make available certain writers to English poets and readers. Hofmann's pre-emptive claim that 'I am not interested in making a sort of Arcimboldo self-portrait made of book reviews' was a red rag to a bull, as far as I was concerned. In fact, of all writers Hofmann seems peculiarly prone to this sort of treatment, because the accumulation of sources into a persona mimics the rather more nuanced way in which writers accumulate influences into a mature and distinctive style. If you don't quite get a Hofmann by adding one part each of Lowell, Benn, Montale, Paulin, Dix, Roth, etc, it's worthwhile spending a few hundred hours pondering over the recipe. To read Hofmann attentively, following up the sources, provided me with a chaotic education, an initiation as it seemed into another person's mind. I began to imagine that a little MH had set up camp in the back of my mind – a mischievous conscience telling me to read more, read better, try harder. And keep an eye on the history around myself.

from Lives of the Poet

ALAN JENKINS

[Numbers 14, 20 and 27 are from the prose of Michael Hofmann]

9

He remembers lunchtime readings at The Swan,
The Dove, The Mermaid; 'the girls were all gazelles'
and among them sat that lovely, dutiful daughter . . .
He loved her. He began to write ghazals
to her eyes that reminded him of the sea . . .
He stepped out to sun that glittered on the water
beyond shop-girls and typists, suited types
and he felt, not that they were 'free bloody birds'
but that happiness might still be caught, endlessly –
a salt-wet happiness in which there were few words,
in which she lay naked with that just-fucked look
and oleanders rustled in the breeze that shook
a leaf-shower down outside, while on
her shoulder shuttered moonlight fell in stripes . . .

62

14

The element of backroom, exile, spit and sawdust,
the secret sorrow, the camouflage jacket,
the disappointed bookstore-manager
and the dozen nutcas – sorry, poetry lovers,
the wallowing in guilt and panic, writing poems
no one realistically wants, for publishers
as hard up as he is, a sort of lemming
among lemmings, assiduous and ineffectual,
gallant and passionate – a kisser of hands
and a kisser of feet, a kisser of arses –
a grievously disappointed and multiply broken man
who somehow continues to align himself
toward the beautiful and the true – he drinks
to dull his nerves, and writes to understand the world.

16

Seeing secretaries in their foreign lunch hours
stretched on the beach or on the sun-warmed earth
of parks, under tattered municipal palms –
he can feel the softness of those tropic airs,
he can hear sea-music, sirens singing,
gentle ukulele songs; he smells tropical flowers,
he can taste the *tristesse* of a tropical berth,
a warm wind from the barrier reef bringing
sticky-sweet of booze, salt that is uniquely theirs;
he can hear that wet *click-click*, a metronome,
the little curling breakers' whisper, *Shush, shush*
as they collapse in foam; can see the tattoos
just below the panty-line, above the bush –
island, palm; a sweat-sheen on their outflung arms.

20

Immoderation, intransigence, exorbitance,
a feeling of being out-of-this-world
or better-than-this-world, the prizes coming
at the wrong times to the proper people
and vice-versa, the protestations
of cheerfulness, the all-pervasive insecurity,
the chronic lack of commitment, the lifelong
dependence on others – for hospitality,
money, love – the simultaneous contradictory
impulses to be adored and alone, connected
and adrift; the brief passionate flare-ups, the long
epistolary retreats, the ecstatic arrivals,
panic departures; 'agonizing reappraisal',
disavowal; severe gloom, habitual dejection.

22

Another funeral, the third or fourth
in as many months – they are falling fast,
the old men, the poets and the scholars
who spent their lives in colleges up north
or book-filled cottages, their knowledge worn like tweed
to hide the drink-stains, frayed sleeves and collars
it did not hide. They have become the past
to boys and girls in school; whoever reads them
now, would not guess what they used to need
to keep them going, sane if not sober –
the muses and disciples, rival cliques –
or the solitudes, white nights and lost weeks . . .
I am only drunk twice a year: June to October,
November to May – his self-love needs them.

At best, a character cameo, an eccentric,
a specialist — no big parts to fill an evening with;
the poet as psycho-pharmaceutical centrifuge,
as astral phenomenon, giving one a sense
of distance, disorderliness and unconventional
possibilities, leaving behind deeper darkness,
humdrum and disapproval; the long doldrums
of his life, the impatience for eternity,
frustration, delay, ambition, self-destructiveness;
a doped athlete or sports coach — exhaustion
and coarseness, a terrible, scandalous confusion —
one might as well go pot-holing or rock-climbing . . .
A little indignant humour, the last
vestiges of decades of rage and denial.

Michael Hofmann: Information Technology

ROSANNA WARREN

One problem for any poem is how to turn information into symbolic form. The challenge is particularly acute for poets whose raw material includes diaristic and journalistic notation, jottings from the quotidian, data that can give an air of unliterary freshness but that threaten to sink a poem into a prosy muck of TMI (or Too Much Information). Michael Hofmann is a great transformer of such debris. How does he pull it off?

He draws his rubbish of the real both from autobiographical and from historical or general-cultural sources, composing his volumes to direct the flow of attention back and forth between these personal and impersonal realms so that the contaminations of family life or erotic experience appear touched by larger disorders: wasted landscapes, political corruption, historical violence. In this imaginative ordering, as in other techniques, he learned a great deal from Robert Lowell; and one of the inspirations in reading early Hofmann is to see him adapting devices from Lowell and turning them, with increasing intensity, to his own purposes. In the generation of poets beginning to publish right after Lowell's death, Hofmann stands quite alone in his relation to that elder: he neither ignored him as so many did, preferring Bishop's less threatening casualness and modesty, nor did he doom himself to semi-conscious pastiche. He took from *Life Studies*, *For the Union Dead*, *History*, *The Dolphin*, and *Day by Day* a certain kind of subject matter and posture in relation to these subjects: personal life detached from the personal and laid out in the lab for examination ('examining and then examining / what I really have against myself': Lowell, 'Redcliffe Square' in *The Dolphin*), combined with the sense, so natural for Lowell with his genealogy, that the individual psyche signifies in the context of history largely conceived.

But subject matter is poetry's least interesting concern. What matters is the 'how'. Three gestures, almost stylistic tics, that the younger poet lifted from Lowell and made his own are strongly on view in early Hofmann, and considering them helps one see how his poems work their extraordinary metamorphoses: ellipses, epigrams, and strings of adjectives. Even as we read Hofmann with Lowell in mind, however, we have to remember the obvious, that a powerful style, a true style, derives from a multiplicity of sources greater and more subtly combined than any supercomputer could count. Hofmann, for instance, has been as nourished by German poetry – by Brecht, Benn, and Eich, among others – as by poems in English. Furthermore, many crucial sources are extra-literary. 'Why should you leave the lamp / Burning alone beside an open book, / And trace these characters upon the sands? / A style is found by sedentary toil / And by the imitation of great masters,' declares 'Hic' in Yeats's 'Ego Dominus Tuus'. To which 'Ille' replies: 'Because I seek an image, not a book.'

Yet Lowell distinctively marks early Hofmann. Consider the ellipses. Lowell so often employed the typographical dot-dot-dots that they became a kind of signature. 'The hospital. My twentieth in twenty years . . .' ('Redcliffe Square'). 'No one had died there in my lifetime . . .' ('My Last Afternoon with Uncle Devereux Winslow', from *Life Studies*). The dots don't serve a single purpose for him, of course, but they often seem a stage direction as to tone of voice, signaling a gracious, even patrician hesitation to declare something too emphatically. In some contexts, they suggest the psychic vulnerability of the speaker, someone whose experience has fractured his utterance and who lets his voice trail off. At the same time, Lowell's ellipses reflect a more general Modernist attitude to material, one of many types of short cuts and suppressions of discursive links.

Like Lowell, Hofmann often uses the typographical ellipsis and the dash in the same poem, and sometimes – as in 'Dean Point' from *Corona, Corona* – in the same sentence: 'It was some kind of quarry, a great excavation – / caterpillar treads, surface water, lumps of clay, / the mess of possibilities . . .' Both forms of punctuation signal a break in the sentence, but they impose drastically different tempi. Whereas the dash speeds things up, betraying excitement, anticipation, and a somersaulting forward into the sense to come, and may imply as well a logical connection between earlier and later statements, the ellipsis retards the utterance and opens a space in which the reader is invited to daydream ('the mess of possibilities . . .'). If Hofmann's ellipses don't have the patrician intonation of Lowell's, they are soft-spoken and aligned with a poetics of cool understatement, irony, and suggestion. At times they carry the narrative forward silently, as in this line from 'The Late Richard Dadd, 1817–1886' from *Corona, Corona*, one of Hofmann's more oblique poems about fathers and sons: 'He had outlived himself at twenty-six . . .' – where the dots stand in for Dadd's forty-three years incarcerated in Bethlem Hospital. (The sons reflect one another: Dadd, too aptly named, the Victorian painter of fairies, who notoriously cut his father's throat; and Michael Hofmann, son of the German novelist Gert Hofmann whose vagaries as adulterous husband and sublimely self-absorbed father are recorded in the poems of *Acrimony* and *Approximately Nowhere*.) The dash, by the way, also has a witty, mimetic role to play in the Dadd poem, in which the painter has drawn his friends 'all with their throats cut'. The punctuation mark cuts the throat of the line: 'The route from Marseille went as the crow flies – / precipitately, a dash from ear to ear.'

The epigram, a concise statement of a general nature, might seem to belong, generically, to a pre-Modernist poetics, but used as a non-sequitur, as often in Lowell, it can be like a pistol shot, a form of abruptness. And it yanks a poem back from a catalogue of particulars that could threaten to dissolve into discrete bits of information: 'The apple was more human there than here', from 'Florence', in *For the Union Dead*. These curt, general declarations occur more often in early Hofmann than in *Corona, Corona* (1993), as Hofmann insists increasingly on specificity and concreteness. They are notable in *Acrimony*. 'Eclogue' opens, 'Industry undressing in front of Agriculture – / not a pretty sight' (a scene both specific and general). 'Nighthawks' opens, 'Time isn't money, at our age, it's water.' As Hofmann relies less on this gesture, the poems devise other ways, including an architecture of symbolic juxtaposition, to avoid frittering into a mess of particulars.

It is in stringing his triads or foursomes of adjectives that Hofmann most closely imitates Lowell and risks displaying himself as ephebe. Lowell's adjectives are famous: one remembers 'Hairy, muscular, suburban', and 'Flabby, bald, lobotomized', both from 'Memories of West Street and Lepke' from *Life Studies*. The filiation is particularly suggestive in the father-son poems. In poem after poem as well as in his prose memoir, Lowell puts his father on trial, dramatizing the patriarch's weakness and foolishness and his own rebellion and guilt: 'I struck my father; later my apology / hardly scratched the surface of his invisible / coronary . . . never to be effaced' ('Mother and Father I', from *History*. Now there is an eloquent ellipsis, charged with unarticulated guilt and mystery: was the apology effective, 'never to be effaced'? Or was the apology ineffective, hardly scratching the surface of the father's weakness – and therefore it's the memory of the father's coronary that's never to be effaced?)

Hofmann, in Part II of *Acrimony* entitled 'My Father's House' and in Part I of *Approximately Nowhere*, anatomizes his relations with his writer father in poems that are, by turns, complicit, yearning, accusatory, pained, and forgiving: 'Who could have said we belonged together, / my father and myself?' ('My Father's House Has Many Mansions', *Acrimony*). In Hofmann's early poems, Lowell the imaginary parricide-poet is perhaps the counter-father who helps give birth to Hofmann's own poems about the elder Hofmann. But by the end of *Acrimony*, Hofmann, unlike Lowell, identifies with his frightening, distant, but powerful father: 'Father, the writer bird writes bird's nest soup – / a frail, disciplined structure, spun from its spittle' ('Old Firm'). If the weak father/powerful son pair of Lowell père et fils threatened to flip into a weak son/powerful father pair in Hofmann, the end of *Acrimony* undoes that equation, as do the moving elegies for Gert Hofmann in *Approximately Nowhere*. Lowell has spectrally touched Hofmann's adjective strings: 'I wanted to share your life. // . . . meet your girlfriends, short-haired, dark, oral' ('My Father's House Has Many Mansions'); 'It was like your signature, / a rapid scrawl from the side of your pen – / individual, overwhelming, impossible – ' ('Bärli'); 'Perplexed, wounded, without confidence, I left him to himself' ('Author, Author'). The signatures here are perhaps less those of Gert Hofmann than of Lowell. But Michael Hofmann the writer is not overwhelmed.

Corona, Corona is composed of three untitled sections. The first presents poems with impersonal, historical subjects, often in the form of biographical portraits: 'Lament for Crassus', 'The Late Richard Dadd, 1817–1886', 'Max Beckmann, 1915'. The second uses apparently autobiographical material, placing an 'I' as a periscope for observed experience, while the poems of the third add up to an acidic travel diary from Mexico. Two poems that mirror one another formally provide good evidence for pondering how Hofmann turns a set of concrete particulars, data, into symbolic shapes. Both 'Biology' from Section I and 'Pastorale' from Section II are built with five unrhymed couplets in free verse. Both are chock-a-block full of information, observations quite external to the speaker/viewer. Both are mysteriously charged with feeling.

Why couplets? They are the only poems in that form in the

book: the other poems in *Corona, Corona* work in tercets, quatrains, quintains, or longer verse paragraphs. In these two poems, which don't tell stories the way many of the other poems do, the couplets create a special terseness in an already concentrated and elliptical style. The pause after each pair of lines enlarges the focus; zooms in, so to speak, on the images presented; and demands meditation. It also demands imagination, since these poems are not forthcoming about what they mean, or how.

'Biology' opens with a view of a nineteenth-century museum: 'The brick ship of Victorian science / steamed on, ivy beard, iron beams and stairs,/ iron paddleboat pillars . . .' One notes, first, a tension between the title and the poem. Modern biology will be at odds with the nineteenth-century descriptive science on display in the Victorian Museum whimsically imagined as 'the brick ship'. (The collection suggests the Museum of Comparative Zoology at Harvard with its famous glass flowers made by the father-and-son team of Leopold and Rudoloph Blaschka, but Hofmann refuses to let that amount of historical specificity enter the poem). The older science is presented in the persons of the whiskery Germans, father and son (like Hofmann father and son?) who knew how to fix the degeneration of fruit in glass, but that very effort to arrest a natural process of decay is doomed, as the poem knows. The more sophisticated biology of the title works against the preservative vision of the museum and its exhibits. But the poem itself is a miniature museum, preserving in its tight couplets both the memory of an older science and the process of its undoing, the ironic play between 'fixing' and 'degenerative'.

Both the dash and the ellipsis are pressed into service for this poem's un-Lowellian purposes. A sentence fragment describing the diseased fruit occupies the center: 'A split blue peach, a bough laden with gangrene − / all pocked, opaque, Venetian, venereal . . .' The dash after 'gangrene' enacts something of the violence splitting the peach, while the dots after 'venereal' open that quartet of adjectives into a huge imaginary space. From the physical aspects of the fruit ('pocked, opaque') we are launched to the far-away realms of 'Venetian, venereal', with connotations of the Venetian art of glass-blowing, decadence, famous courtesans, and STDs. The poem is scrupulously non-metrical – as unwilling to sustain the illusion of nineteenth-century lyric poetics as of nineteenth-century science? – but lavish in its phonetic play. This dreaming line insists on its symmetrical sound patterns in alliteration and assonance: POCKed OPAQue/ VENEtian VENEREal. The four adjectives are followed by four nouns describing the general and desiccated texture of the museum ('dry air, manila light, cardboard and silence'), preparing for the final couplet, which announces, in its incontrovertible future indicative, the time when the illusions of the exhibits will have failed.

In its terse, objective, minimalist, and impersonal way, 'Biology' replays the great lyric themes of Time and Illusion ('That time of year thou mays't in me behold . . .'), but almost removes eros from the equation. Almost, but not quite. There at the heart of the poem fester 'Venetian, venereal', hinting at love's sickly appetite: 'My love is as a fever, longing still / For that which longer nurseth the disease . . .'

No first person pronoun gave us a point of view in 'Biology', but in the single sentence of 'Pastorale' perspective is controlled by an 'I', a 'slewed census-taker' who walks and observes. The poem opens: 'Where the cars razored past on the blue highway, / I walked, unreasonably, contre-sens . . .' While 'Biology' had dimly in its memory a tradition of erotic lyric, 'Pastorale' punishes a long tradition of lyric idealization of nature. Hofmann dedicates the poem to the Swiss novelist Beat Sterchi, whose novel *Cow* (which Hofmann translated into English) recounts the life of a sensuous, gentle cow from her youth in high meadows to her ghoulish death in an urban slaughterhouse, witnessed by the immigrant Spanish laborer who had once cared for her.

The dedication plunges us into a world of nature betrayed and uglified by humans. Slightly more metrical than 'Biology' – one can make out five stresses, though certainly not in regular feet, in many of these lines – 'Pastorale' maintains, on the one hand, a cool demeanor as it notes the dead animals and trash along the highway, and on the other hand indulges in a mischievous euphoria of rhyme, alliteration, and assonance: Feminax/anthrax, flattened rat/floribund, stockpiled flocks/blocks, ancillary/bacillary . . .

'Pastorale' is an ars poetica, a portrait of the poet as someone positioned contre-sens, in opposition, against the traffic of a violent, wasteful and poisonous culture. He is an observer, a census-taker 'slewed', no doubt, as in turned or swung around, by the tailwind of the cars razoring past, by industrial modernity. What he observes has already become a kind of writing: 'cursive snout' of the crushed rat. In this desolate landscape of agribusiness, where haystacks have been 'stockpiled' in plastic wrap as if they were an arsenal of biochemical weapons and where human female fertility means only pain to be controlled by drugs (Feminax), the memory of classical pastoral survives only in the phrase 'green verge'. But any vestige of Virgilian pastures, Shakespearean greenwood, or Miltonic wild Thyme and the gadding Vine o'ergrown has corrupted into a nightmare. The animals have taken on the metallic quality of the civilization that has flattened them, the bullet-copper and bullet-steel of pheasants – and the vegetation, the floribund ivy not to mention those sinister hayrolls, seems Bosch-like in its excess.

'Biology' and 'Pastorale' both meditate obliquely (and bleakly) on art in the world, with an equal emphasis on both terms. In 'Biology', glass artists had tried, like Shakespeare in the sonnets, to preserve the fugitive course of life, and Hofmann is another such glass artist, 'fixing' the degeneration of an older science, an older poetic art, feelings and knowledge. 'Pastorale', like many other Hofmann poems, depicts a landscape ruined by human greed. The poem that follows it in *Corona, Corona*, 'On the Beach at Thorpeness', extends the destructive inventory to include a nuclear plant and 'roaring waves of fighters headed back to Bentwaters'. The sea recites a litany of disaster: 'Jaw jaw. War war.' Beneath their appearance of journalistic notation, Hofmann's poems organize experience with a fierce selectivity of detail, implied arguments all the more powerful for being delivered sotto voce, and high-adrenaline sound patterns. He learned what he needed to learn from various masters – Lowell among them – and turned it all to a voice and vision unmistakably his own.

Sad to say, the vision is also ours, and we would ignore it at our peril. This ruining land is where we live. So does subject matter 'matter', after all? Yes, it does. But only if art has made it matter; if it has become real in language. Michael Hofmann is that kind of necessary poet who presents a new and convincing version of the real.

Camelot in Florida

ERIC BLIMAN

'Stray nooses of wisteria
toss purposefully, aimlessly, who can say.'
– Michael Hofmann

You kept an unabridged dictionary
on our oval conference table in Turlington –
our long, lopsided oaken slice of Camelot –
as if to keep certainty on display.
Often, we needed a brighter definition

to help light our way through Brodsky's
Collected, or *Montale in English*,
or to help root out a god forgotten
by all but two or three of us Argus-eyed
ironists, young monsters from the burbs.

Any guilty, interested party,
such as me on more than one occasion,
could check the finer points of his own gaffe,
squint at its thin-type etymology, its correct
pronunciation. The dictionary swiveled.

How we murdered English, your beloved,
adoptive language. Does the *OED*
remind us not to repeat our mistakes?
Can one stumble and still make one's way?
Aimlessly, purposefully. Who can say?

Turlington Hall, Third Floor

CURTIS D'COSTA

I have my notes from Michael Hofmann's poetry workshop in front of me. They date from spring 2008. Every Monday night ten of us would meet in the Creative Writing Suite on the third floor of Turlington Hall. We sat in swivel chairs around a long table, surrounded by herons and alligators on University of Florida Writers' Festival posters dating back to the 80s. Michael presided at the head. He was always ready to begin early. That semester he grew a beard, and I remember the watch with a black leather band and gold-trimmed face he always wore. The photographs I've seen of him capture his alertness. Sitting in a high-backed conference room chair, he has the look of someone who's just hopped off a bike.

I remember listening to him talk about poems and feeling overwhelmed by the sheer amount of decisions the business of writing well seemed to involve. Who knew, for example, there was a name and literary function for what at first glance appears to be mere gossip: praeteritio? Most of my notes are quotations of things he said, short, ample, inventive phrases that call to mind Joan Didion's definition of notes from her essay 'On Keeping a Notebook': 'bits of the mind's string too short to use'. He said *Hunger* by Knut Hamsun was his favorite novel. I put it down and marvelled at the perspicacity of his other comment about the book: 'no eating, no input'. MacNeice's *Autumn Journal* he brilliantly called 'a film with voice-over'. It would not be the only time he drew on audio to explain how poems worked: Hugo Williams's are 'clever, pop-songy, modest'; Lowell is 'a poet with a brass section' who treated 'stanzas like playing cards'; and Schuyler's improvisational 'October' reminded him of Satie, 'playable with one hand, going nowhere while getting there'.

We had some laughs too. Our captain confessed he expected a poem about some dear old ladies when he first came across Schuyler's 'Korean Mums'. Then there was the time a slinky appeared in one of our poems. Michael objected and someone wanted to know why. After mulling it over a bit, he told us about an old radio show in the UK where a contestant said any word he'd like, his opponent said any word she'd like, and so on, until one of them cracked up laughing. 'Slinky', he argued, would win every time, and words like that don't belong in our poems.

On the first day of the workshop I had taken the previous year, William Logan handed around copies of 'Freebird' and then delivered it in his radio-friendly baritone. It was the first time I had heard one of Michael's poems read aloud and it changed my perspective. William Logan lectures with his fists, drawing circles with them as he talks, and if 'Freebird' wasn't intimidating before, after that it was raw power.

My first encounter with Michael in person had also been intimidating. As a formal department function was winding down one night, my classmates started talking about dreams. Michael was still around. Hoping to strike up a conversation and introduce myself, I asked him if he had ever dreamed up a sentence or line in his sleep and written it down the next day. It seemed he hadn't heard me, so I asked him again. Finally he said – in the same indignant way his father, I imagined, had said it to Ted Hughes, according to Michael's poem 'Cheltenham' – 'No.' Then he said he had to leave.

So when I wrote him an email a month later proposing to take a reading tutorial with him covering twentieth-century German poetry, I wasn't expecting his swift, enthusiastic reply. Slowly I read his anthology over two weeks. The spine has since come unglued, yet I refuse to replace it, in that sentimental, hipster way people cling to frayed, awesome things they wish they'd been the first to discover. An anthology of German poetry that represents Wordsworth's 'My heart leaps up when I behold' as an English translation has to be wonderful. On the left-hand page reserved for the original German is Ernst Jandl's surface translation, which is a transliteration of the English. A translation of the surface translation appears in a footnote, topping it off. And so a trio performs on two pages a set where 'a rainbow in the sky' becomes 'er renn bohr in sees kai', translated back as 'he runs drill in lake's quay'.

Before I knew it I had spent a sizeable portion of my MFA career on a large, Southern-style porch with Joseph Roth's novels and articles, Michael's translations. But when we talked about them, we talked Roth, just as we spoke of the poets' poetry when talking about his translations of Rilke, Benn, Inge Müller, and Günter Eich. In an interview from 1999 he called translating 'a mental fight' whose object is to provide an experience. But for whom? Does a translator write for a bilingual audience as well? And if so, does he write for himself? What experience is he left with? I couldn't say his love of Roth eclipsed his pride in having translated him so well. I couldn't even say he translated Roth well, ignorant as I am of German. What I could sense was that these authors somehow were now his, his to share, his to celebrate: perhaps even his to be.

Quizzically, Michael Hofmann

SUZANNE ZWEIZIG

Michael Hofmann was not your usual teacher. He didn't lecture, had only the most modest sense of authority in the classroom, often winged it (sometimes to brilliant effect, other times not) and sometimes struggled on the spot to convey his intuitive sense of literature and language in words. Rather than expound upon a subject, Michael's mode was the one-liner, sometimes delivered after what seemed like moments of silent thought. He assigned us novels in poetry workshops, rarely made formal syllabi, and expected us to engage deeply with the material – as he himself did – without being prompted. Those who wanted more direction were occasionally frustrated. Outside of class, Michael was a great favorite. His genius was widely recognized; he was fun-loving, kind, always went for a drink after workshop, had an ever-open door for a literary chat, and was quirky enough to delight us in an absent-minded professor kind of way with his tendency to overlook (purposely? I was never quite sure) life's tedious practicalities in his focus on literary pursuits. One year we sat waiting an hour for Michael to show up to our first class of the semester, only to learn later that he hadn't gotten his US visa on time, so hadn't gotten on the plane. 'Honey, you could have called!' we might have said, like the wife left stranded with a ruined dinner. But these mishaps became part of his legend and seemed evidence that he lived in a rarefied air. Then of course, there was the British accent, which is always a hit in the States. The women all had crushes on Michael, and I won't quite say the men all wanted to be him, but I will report that three of my male colleagues, inspired by one of Michael's sartorial choices, all bought seersucker trousers at a local outlet and sat around wearing them one night.

Sorting through some old papers recently, I found a copy of a lecture on Durs Grünbein that Michael had given at a literary conference sometime during the years I was a student at Florida. He had placed it in my mailbox one day in response to conversations we had been having about German poetry and translation. Rediscovering it these years later, I had to smile and wonder at it again, just as I had then – not, admittedly, for the content, which is profound and itself worth several essays – but rather for the note Michael had scrawled in black ink on the top margin of the first page: 'For S.Z., quizzically, Michael Hofmann'.

At the time I remember thinking it a funny word choice – somewhat charming, a bit quaint, but also . . . well, curious. I remember standing in the English Department mailroom examining the script from various angles, trying to figure out if 'quizzically' was indeed the word Michael had intended (his handwriting could be difficult to decipher). At home, I studied it more. Once all other possibilities had been eliminated and it remained 'Quizzically', I wrestled with the larger question of whatever did Michael mean by it? That would have been around 2003, when Michael was working intensively on the poems for *Ashes for Breakfast*, undertaking the task of translating Grünbein's poetry after years of translating German prose. The lecture expresses his thoughts about the endeavor, which have since been published in other places with equal finesse, intelligence and wit. So why, then, quizzical? Was he unsure? Did he want my opinion on the piece? Part of me wanted to be so flattered.

Unearthing the manuscript these years later, I found myself going through the same mental maneuvers as my student self did, puzzling again first over the handwriting, then the word itself and then its implications. Admittedly, the word is a simple gesture, perhaps not more than a whimsical moment on Michael's part, but I keep coming back to it. Truth is, he was quizzical – about what I thought, about what all his students thought. His mind didn't come into the classroom with conclusions, as much as questions, not so much to convey ideas about literature as to engage in them with us. This isn't to say Michael didn't have a solid base of learning and strong aesthetic principles to offer. He did, and he did. His 'street cred' in this regard was unassailable and requires no defense; however, he didn't seem to be as much interested in repeating what he knew as in examining and expanding it, and the classroom offered another place for him to do that. A one-way passage of ideas from him to us would have been unthinkable to him, and although many teachers would claim, especially at the graduate school level, that teaching should be a two-way exchange, I have rarely met anyone who embodied this attitude quite as much as Michael in both demeanor and action.

Part of his attitude rested in letting go of (the illusion of) authority, for despite Michael's prodigious learning and reading, he was always open to thinking about even the most basic poetic concepts afresh, embracing exceptions, and rarely ever took conventional wisdom about poetry for granted. He was one of the few teachers who, upon being asked a difficult question (for example 'What is poetry?', which I asked him once), allowed himself to say with absolute sincerity, 'I don't know.' He'd look away for a few minutes in deep reflection, as if he, too, didn't get it, then offer a tentative thought or two (usually nothing too shabby!) and shrug. But the conversation would not end there; sometimes weeks later, in another conversation, Michael would come back to the point and throw another idea into the pot, which had obviously been simmering: 'You know when you asked me about poetry the other week . . .' he'd say. And so answers would be pieced together bit by bit over months, a sentence at a time, tentatively. This dynamic is what made it so rewarding to ask Michael the difficult questions: you weren't shut down with an answer before the fun of thinking was over.

Indeed, a lot of the assignments Michael brought into our class-rooms seemed as much for him to work things out as for us. I will never forget, for example, the very first poetry workshop I took with Michael, in which he taught novels instead of poetry, an experiment he always wanted to try, he confessed, because he was interested in what poets might learn from prose writers. Not content with his own rationale, however, he asked each of us, as we went around the room introducing ourselves that first day, to say what we thought of the idea and how we thought the novels might influence our study of poetry. I don't remember exactly how I responded, but I do remember saying that I always imagined I'd be writing novels, not poetry, to which Michael responded emphatically, 'Me *too.*'

I'm not sure our class ever came to profound insights about poetry by reading novels that semester, but it was the start of something. Talking to Michael in his office once, I asked him why he liked those particular novels, a question he pondered and finally answered simply 'Because of the sentences, I think.' This surprised me; I had never heard anybody like a novel pure-ly for the sentences before, but eventually it made perfect sense as I became more fully cognizant of Michael's finely honed style – both poetic and prose. Some two years later I sat in on a poetry workshop as Michael taught yet another novel, Malcolm Lowry's *Under the Volcano*, one of his great loves. ('It's one of those books you pull off your shelf at least once a year, open up to a page and start reading,' he said). A novel of epic proportions – madness and alcoholism – it nonetheless fascinated Michael not for that large-scale drama but for the sentences and patterns of movement – the way Lowry built his world using the smallest components. More than the content of the discussion, I remember the pace, which went in fits and starts. Michael would ponder something aloud then wait to see, based on our responses, if anybody was in his intellectual neighborhood. Some students would pick up his thread, others would stray into tangents about who played whom in the movie; occasionally Michael would loop back to his original musings, looking for stragglers who might pick up on them. Myself, I remember feeling as if I were finally able to penetrate beyond the traditional English major perspective of theme/character/allusions and get a glimpse into how Michael saw the book: almost like an architectural structure of patterns composed at the finest level, sentences being just one of them. In truth, I still have many questions and much more thinking to do about this (quizzically!), but good questions may be the best legacy a teacher can leave you.

I once asked Michael if he liked teaching and was surprised by his unequivocal yes, partly because so many other writers I knew complained that teaching infringed on their 'writing time' and partly because Michael himself tended to dislike real-world obligations. But I don't think Michael saw working with students as antithetical to his literary pursuits. On one hand, he was such a 'work horse', as one of my classmates described him – toiling away through the night on his own material – that his primetime was pretty fortified against infringements. But more importantly, I had the sense that Michael's classroom was not really time away from his 'own work', rather an incubator for it. Indeed, in some of Michael's publications over the last few years, I am thrilled to recognize ideas that were a-brew in our classrooms: an edited collection of Malcolm Lowry's 'other work', for example, and, in the scant selection of new poems, a dystopian 'Idyll', a form he once had us try our hands at, bringing in odd, eclectic samples of idylls to inspire us.

Indeed, Michael was fully engaged in our little community of writers in Florida. It was always livelier in spring semester when he was in town: he came to all our readings and department events, laughed at our antics and egged us on in his own introverted way with the occasional one-liner, retaining a public-school boy sense of humor and lingo that he would bring out to comic effect: 'Strawberry Ripple,' he once pronounced, as a blond woman with red streaks in her hair walked by the coffee shop where we were sitting. Amid all of this, you could turn to him any time at any function, no matter how raucous, ask him a question about a writer, and he would switch gears, becoming thoughtful and immediately engaged in the topic.

When I saw Michael last (almost two years now) for a visit in Florida, he had gone to full-time status and seemed happy about it, telling me all the news about the program. During the visit I spoke to him about, among other things, teaching, a profession I have not chosen partly because I am uncomfortable with the idea of being taken as the authority on a poem and pronouncing it good or bad. Michael dismissed my fears. 'Students will know – or they will learn – that you're not. That's part of it.'

Wunderkind

ANDRÉ NAFFIS-SAHELY

Unshaven and barefoot, as if on a pilgrimage.
His house is blue: the walls, the carpet, the cups;
the kind of blue you see in sad monasteries,

the paint veined and peeling, with brittle bits of gold
hanging on in the rims. Like Gottfried Benn –
a spiritual father figure – he likes to stay home:

where the coffee is better and there is no small-talk.
He seems scattered, has lost a book somewhere:
a translation. All his life he has hidden a language,

now he eats, breathes and interprets it. Later,
our awkwardness spilled over Hampstead Heath,
where we walked, mostly in silence. We had soup

and beer around the corner, then took a short-cut
to the bus stop, and he was gone; brought by the wind,
taken back by it: the soft-spoken wunderkind of despair.

Give the Moment

MARY BETH FERDA

By the time I met Michael, in the second term of my first year at the University of Florida, I wasn't the only student who had begun thinking of my work as divided between 'workshop poems' (those I wrote to satisfy class requirements) and 'my poems' (the 'real' work I did on my own time, confronting whatever actually interested or obsessed me, without the looming image of my workshop audience). I remember students trading hastily made-up writing prompts before leaving for Christmas break, else they might produce nothing new in that first month spent away from the workshop. After the holiday, Michael came to town to teach spring term. One didn't have to write anything '*for* Michael' as I felt I did with other teachers over the years. He never handed out an assignment or gave a prompt. I was left with no choice but to give in to what obsessed me – write a 'real' poem – and show it to everyone.

For better or for worse, Michael treated me like I knew what I was doing. His idea of leading a workshop, as I experienced it, was to painstakingly choose a small, focused reading list, then show up every week to reflect on a text with us and see what happened. If something we were reading launched a poem for any of us, fine. If we felt like bringing that poem into the workshop, great. Something about this loose format – the spontaneity, its implied faith that all we had to do was get together with our heads over the same book and something would happen – seemed magical, intimate. I spent much of my class time with Michael sitting at a round table, watching him with his chin in one hand, then the other, quiet and deep into a poem. Long pauses would pass while Michael chewed on a text, while the rest of us were supposedly chewing on it too. I wasn't chewing; often, I was watching Michael chew, my pen poised, waiting for that moment when, finally, he would open his mouth to strike at the essence of a line, or an image, or an entire piece – Michael never talked *around* anything. In this way, listening to Michael is like reading Michael. I noted his (complete) response to one student's poem: 'There's a sense of things falling over themselves to get into the poem and mean something . . . to bring feelings and talk about them, but not talk about them very much. *Give the moment* (this underlined in my notes) . . . I absolutely believe in the moment.'

Michael, of course, was not given to making comments for the sake of commenting. When he liked a poem, he might say, 'I think it's magnificent' and that was that. When he disliked a poem, one I'd spent countless hours on, hoping to include it in my master's thesis he was directing, he would say, 'this one I don't think so' with the same nimble finality in his invariably soft voice, and turn to the next page.

The more I tried to *give the moment*, the more I wrote to face what scared or shamed me, the happier he was with my work. I was plagued by doubt, by fear of the impressions given by the honesty I was challenging myself to put forth – fear of how the poems 'made it sound'. I remember one teacher telling me that a poem about my mother was 'profoundly depressing', a reaction I found disheartening in its simplicity. Michael was irritated. 'That is an infantile reaction to art.' He went on to say, 'Don't worry. You continue to produce these things and they continue to make you nervous . . . Be of good heart.'

That's typically how we parted, with a hug and his reminder to 'be of good heart'. Often, when I think of Michael now, I am hearing those words. Sometimes his reminder sounded like a question. *Be of good heart, will you? I believe in this work you're doing. Do you? Or don't you?*

I've been reading Michael a lot in the past few weeks, and I don't feel so far away. That's because, I think, when you read Michael, you get the real Michael. When you receive a note from Michael, it's signed, *Ever, Michael*. When you see Michael, no matter where or why, you get the real Michael, his sweetness and curiosity coming through in the utter absence of small talk, the assumed mutual interest in only the gritty details. Michael is ever the authentic Michael Hofmann. And authenticity is all he really asked of me – that I might have the heart to face my moment and become a believer.

Verloren und Gefunden

Gray batting rolled in off the Channel,
the rough breeze catching on birches
whose papery bark looked American.
Who would want to kill in such a place?

The moon lay just visible through a rip in clouds,
lazy, inconsolable,
like a man's cheek scraped bare.
The scatter of pink petals was your entourage,

passive and willing to do anything for you.
What was fitting except what was unfitting?
Worked over, corroded, rusty bell-metal,
the sky stood like a jar, ostentatious, unostentatious.

At twenty, left luggage along the Cam.
At fifty-five, you sat in your old language
like a conqueror, as if you had grown another tongue.
What wounds the elegy is merely retrospective.

The lake lay, a silver sheet after beaten rain.
The canvas covered what eyesight could not.
There you were, on the far shore,
at home everywhere, nowhere.

Fugitive Pieces

CHARLES BOYLE

Sometime after the Wall came down – but not long after: Gert Hofmann died in 1993 – there was a BBC arts programme in which Michael and his father Gert wander around places (Leipzig?) in East Germany in which his father had lived. The weather is mild. They peer into rooms and, I assume, discuss old times, though I recall nothing of that. In the one scene I do remember the Hofmanns are sitting at a table outside a café and not talking. Maybe they do talk a little, but they prefer not to. There may be coffee, there may be pedestrians passing by. And the camera holds on them to the point where every movement – a hand swept though thinning hair – becomes an event; and then longer, past the point where these movements go back to being non-events, and it's so fine that I want there to be an entire TV channel dedicated to just this continuing scene, though of course a part of its loveliness is my knowing that at any moment the director is going to lose patience and cut.

There's a reference to this programme in a 1999 review by Dennis O'Driscoll of *Approximately Nowhere*, so it wasn't the dream that for a long time I thought it was, having met no one else who had seen it. But I suspect that if I saw the programme again, the scene I'm recalling would clock no more than half a minute, probably less. (Re-reading Penelope Fitzgerald, I find that certain episodes I remember as occupying whole chapters turn out to have been achieved in a couple of paragraphs, a page and a half. In Elizabeth Bowen's *The House in Paris*, Max, Karen and Naomi have a picnic in a Twickenham garden – end of April, but 'warm and idle, like summer' – that I remember as occupying a third of the book: in fact twenty pages, less. There are ways in which a gesture – a flavour, a mood – can represent a life, a few sentences a writer's whole work.)

Recently I did dream that Michael had written a series of three pieces for an Italian newspaper, and that the original English texts were posted online on the website of a US newspaper – but they were behind a paywall, and there were problems with my username and password, and when one of the pieces did finally flash up on the screen the internet connection went down. This was a frustration dream, one of so many, but it was largely true of the way in which new work by Michael filters through to me. There's an occasional poem in *Poetry* (Chicago), an occasional essay/review in the *London Review of Books*. There's a steady flow of translations, an astonishing amount (does he have studio assistants?), many of works by authors I've not previously known of and published by little-known presses, many hardly remarked on. This is hardly Operation Shock and Awe.

In the beginning it was different. Like, I suspect, a number of other contributors here, I first became aware of Michael's poems when they started appearing regularly in the UK magazines; and then the first collection, *Nights in the Iron Hotel* (1983). 'I had just entered on my seventeenth year, when the sonnets of Mr Bowles, twenty in number, and just then published in a quarto pamphlet . . .' – Coleridge speaking, and I was perhaps seventeen myself when I underlined that whole passage in *Biographia Literaria*: 'The great works of past ages seem to a young man things of another race, in respect to which his faculties must remain passive and submiss, even as to the stars and mountains. But the writings of a contemporary, perhaps not many years older than himself, surrounded by the same circumstances, and disciplined by the same manners, possess a reality for him, and inspire an actual friendship as of a man for a man . . . The poems themselves assume the properties of flesh and blood.'

But even then, Michael was betwixt-and-between, gifted with languages and complex mentors from different cultures, and an eye and and an ear that, while taking in the world that was mine, were tuned, compellingly, in a different way. He wasn't German (though born there). He wasn't English (though sent to school here), certainly not in a Betjeman way, and in the end not even in a Conrad way, though it's tempting to invoke an extradition treaty: as recently as last year, George Szirtes wrote, in a sentence that links Michael with a couple of other poets who are English through-and-through, 'I thought there must be a line to be drawn . . . that would define what I loved about English writing, the understatement, the nonsense, the faint desperation and disorientation, the rejection of bombast, the sudden jaggedness of life, and the perfect register of the perfect word, and that this was somehow . . . intrinsically English'. And now, though I believe he lives mostly in America, it's impossible to think of him as American.

Something grounded yet on the wing, elusive . . . There's probably a word for it in German, a word favoured by one of the writers Michael is drawn to translate. Certainly he does himself a favour by not being a paid-up member of the UK culture club. The introduction to *Behind the Lines*, Michael's 2001 collection of 'pieces on writing and pictures', far from being any kind of apology for the kind of miscellany that for many writers is a form of marking time, relishes in a way of writing, and of making a book, that's built up from 'first thoughts and second thoughts, *"flashes" e dediche* in Montale's phrase, flashes and inscriptions, swift, provisional, personal responses . . . a collage, a mosaic, not a bronze or a lump of marble.' It's a form of criticism that mirrors, I suspect, the way much of the writing it addresses comes about. First things: a word, another, a rhythm, a sentence. In interview, Michael has spoken of his obligation as a translator to write 'interesting sentences'. 'I think I go to novelists,' he writes in the introduction to his Malcolm Lowry selection, 'for sentences.' What the sentences may (or may not) add up to – a novel, a poem, an *oeuvre*, a lump of marble – is by the by.

Is it a poet, is it a translator, is it a fish? We like, on the whole, to be told what we're getting, and people charged with introducing Michael at public events often have a category issue: he's this but he's also that. And then Michael will stand and begin to talk or to read in his soft-spoken voice, and someone at the back of the room will shout: 'Speak up!' Small silence, a little shuffling. No. Listen more carefully. His voice – inclusive of pauses, questionings, absolute convictions, and backed by a range of reading that somehow manages to be not daunting but liberating – invariably comes from a place I can't quite place, which itself suggests it's worth attending to. Strangely (I mean wonderfully), that most of his published words have been in the service of others hasn't even dented his individualness. He is tied to no consensus, either in his own work or in his opinions of the work of others. He has been, for me, formative. He works in the way I want my writers to work, even when they're not actually writing, and I'm more than grateful.

Feeding the Baby

MICHAEL SCHMIDT

                    . . . in the end
She fed her vampire everything she had,
Mother and father first, her husband
(In some ways she was glad to see him go);
Then the children one by one by one,
Keeping back, held close under her shawl
Her favourite, in a milky gown, with scowling gums,
Fat-fisted, the pinkest mouthful of all.
When there was nothing left, she fed him
That one too, its salty fingers, china eyes,
Watched his slow jaw work a way right through it,
The baby shrilling a song as babies do
While it could, waving its bloody feet.
The vampire licked his chops and looked right at her.

How much of her was his, was him by now,
Transformed to tissue, then to excrement,
And still he was not hers though she presumed
What she'd provided totalled a nuptial vow.

She had no more to give. The vampire left her
One evening, not moonlit – 'just going to the shops' . . .

'Nothing Dreamier than Barracks!'

JULIAN STANNARD

The novelist Aldo Busi once declared that any self-respecting writer needs to jettison *la tenerezza*. Michael Hofmann had hacked away at easy emotion by the time *Nights in the Iron Hotel* came out in 1983. It was a pretty good start. The prescribed splinter of ice makes its inward journey as effectively as the 'kleine Aster' stitched into the corpse by a medical student in Gottfried Benn's macabre poem. Benn's bleak aesthetic, the aesthetic of the operating table, those 'prankish rearrangements of corpses', is dealt with in a brilliant piece in *Behind the Lines: Pieces on Writing and Pictures* (2001).

Hofmann's 'Diablerie', from *Nights in the Iron Hotel*, is characteristically 'jocular': 'In Your arms / is someone else's child, a black-eyed baby girl / dressed like His Satanic Majesty in a red romper suit; / a gleeful crustacean, executing pincer movements.' 'Diablerie' would seem to prefigure the equally concise 'Vagary' from Hofmann's *Approximately Nowhere* (1999): 'I can really only feign disapproval / of my youngest / dibbling his semolina'd fingers / in the satiny lining of her red coat.' In *Behind the Lines* Hofmann argues that the short poem, 'that daunting form', can look like 'a few bricks falling over one another'. Both these poems are architecturally solid.

Nights in the Iron Hotel is not, in fact, without its own particular brand of gleefulness – 'You move the fifty seven muscles it takes to smile' – as it leads us into never remote, dysfunctional worlds. Sex is always tense, like the Cold War, and subject to negotiations, unless you're the speaker from 'A Western Pastoral': 'I married a woman I found in New Orleans. / . . . / Under the stars, after a business reversal / she puts her head in my lap and empties me.' Sometimes the reader is a voyeur behind a 'leather curtain that hangs in the doorway', and not infrequently, as in the politically savvy title-poem, an 'inability to function' is the main source of fascination. In Hofmann's poetry to be ill at ease, to fall into 'irksome' silence, to experience ennui and disenchantment, to reach out for the 'pessimistic sublime' is cool.

Acrimony – the second book, first published in 1986 and re-launched by Faber in its queasy lemony jacket ('the yellow of unlove'?) at the beginning of the millennium – made an Oedipal study of salami-breathing monsters, tyrannizing bedrooms. The title of the book is a statement of Hofmann's poetic, his carefully cultivated *esthétique du mal*. We suspect things are going to enjoy a dysfunctional verve; in fact we're reminded in 'Ancient Evenings', the opening poem, that gravity is a kind of humour and humour its own form of gravity. The poems in *Acrimony* smile and scowl in cunning ways. One might read Hofmann's poems as a series of brilliant jokes where 'bleakness swings into a kind of exhilaration' and 'heartstopping fun'. It's tempting to go straight to Part Two, 'My Father's House', the scorched heartlands of *Acrimony*, with its accusatory, 'confessional' account of the poet's German father, the novelist Gert Hofmann, 'gone to seed' like a Third World dictator. But the book's opening twenty-five poems are so adept at creating an atmosphere of dandified brutality they are worth celebrating on that score alone.

The organization of the book demarcates Hofmann's Anglo-German cultural background. His points of reference include the Official Raving Loony Monster candidate and the iconic Berlin zoo. Born in Freiburg in 1957, Hofmann came to England in 1961 and was educated in this country, not insignificantly at the six-hundred-year-old Winchester College, which served to inculcate that 'parodic Englishness' he refers to in his *Thumbscrew* interview with Fran Brearton. Like Ford Madox Ford, Hofmann seems at times both quintessentially English and decisively un-English. In the BBC documentary about father and son – *My Father's House* (1990) – we see the poet (almost the *enfant terrible*) reading from *Acrimony* to a group of adolescent boys at Eton. It is as if he were both parodying that acquired Englishness as well as enacting a coup from within. He steps into that bastion of (male) privilege, not completely dissimilar to Winchester College, to un-mask the patriarch and sabotage filial obligation. A concerned youth asks whether the poems might affect the poet's relationship with his parents.

Whereas the poems about the German father are cultural as well as psychoanalytical enquiries, Lowellian in effect, the poems in the first section show Hofmann taking stock of 1980s London, the Thatcherite metropolis (with its enthusiastic embrace of Reaganomics). Critics at the time were quick to see the book as useful contemporary reportage. 'Impotence' shows the poet in 'this London faubourg of service flats, gigolos, black-mail' where 'Gymnasial grunts echo from the Lego barracks: / the Voice of America, and a flag to brighten the dullest day. / The Marines, sombre and muscle-bound – shaved knuckle-heads!' The last verse of 'Nighthawks', in turn, wonders how long the threatened branch-line will survive even as it rattles and screeches 'between the hospital / lit like a toy, and the castellated factory – / a *folie de grandeur* of late capitalism.' But 'Nighthawks' isn't merely chronicle. Although unmistakably anchored in that time, with its nocturnal, infernal 'hamburger heaven', the poem might seem to invoke the 1920s of Otto Dix, one of Hofmann's subjects in *Behind the Lines*.

Reviewing the 1992 retrospective of Dix at the Tate, Hofmann acknowledges the painter's talent for expressing 'social dislocation, impatience, submission, false glitter and the inadequate healing powers of capitalism'. Hence plenty of room for Dix in the late twentieth century. Hofmann draws our attention to Dix's portraits of prostitutes, the set pieces *To Beauty* and *The Metropolis*. What interested Dix (and, palpably, what also interests Dix's late-twentieth-century reviewer) 'was ugliness, which seems [to Dix] almost like a creed'. The ambience of Hofmann's 'Nighthawks' with its street-lighting, its hint of Eliotic fog, its reference to gas, is almost modernistic, even *entre les deux guerres*.

> The derelicts queue twice round the tearoom.
> Outside, the controlled prostitutes move smoothly
> through the shoals of men laughing off their fear.
> The street-lamps are a dull coral, snakes' heads.
>
> Earlier, I watched a couple over your shoulder.
> She was thin, bone-chested, dressed in black lace,
> her best features vines of hair. Blatant, ravenous,
> post-coital, they greased their fingers as they ate.
>
> I met a dim acquaintance, a man with the manner
> of a laughing-gas victim, rich, frightened and jovial.
> Why doesn't everyone wear pink, he squeaked.
> Only a couple of blocks are safe in his world.

'Albion Market', whose title alerts us to the poem's later drift, gives us a medley of contemporary slogans: Arsenal Rules the World, Goodbye, Kilburn, Everything Must Go. The phone booth assiduously caters for the specialist: '"rubber", and "correction" for the incorrigible'. Yet, as night falls over Bayswater, where women dangle their 'most things considered' from the kerb, it's not so difficult to switch louche London for the 'yeasty, nervy' quickening of 1920s Berlin. Bayswater is suddenly informed by Weimar; sadomasochism perfected by British thugs in bowler hats; Albion (with its accretion of perfidy) now bristling in neo-con, post-Bang bondage.

A man came down the street with the meth-pink eyes
of a white rat, his gait a mortal shuffle.

A British bulldog bowler hat clung to his melting skull.
. . . Game spirits, tat and service industries,
an economy stripped to the skin trade. Sex and security,
Arsenal boot boys, white slaves and the SAS.

We might think of the young Bunting – 'Secret, solitary, a spy' – trundling along Tottenham Court Road, mating beauty with squalor. In *Nights in the Iron Hotel* Hofmann calls one of his poems 'De-militarised Zone', a useful trope on that occasion for a process of rapprochement after 'our tired argument in your parked car'. But Hofmann is a poet-critic perennially conscious of borders and military scenarios, even those 'waves of fighters head[ing] back to Bentwaters' ('On the Beach at Thorpeness'). His piece on Gottfried Benn moves from the early *Morgue* poems (1912) to the period Benn was working as an army doctor towards the end of the Second World War. Hofmann cites Benn's own account of that period, the strange peace-in-war, that 'behind-the-lines existence', where behind the dreamy barracks was a secret world of seclusion, 'a kind of béguinage'. The army, for Benn, was an 'aristocratic form of emigration'. In *Acrimony*, Hofmann plays at the role of poet spy, picnicking above the parade ground, flicking ash and wincing at his pips 'going lickety-split, / hitting the deck fifty feet down, among the sentries . . .' ('Entr'acte') Hofmann knows, as if he still had the special vision of the émigré , that behind the lines are where the best lines are to be found.

The Spider's Web, Hofmann reminds us in his piece on Joseph Roth (some of whose lines 'bleed' across the father's desk in 'Fine Adjustments'), 'is set among the bigots, spies, and terrorist militias of Weimar'. Poets of the 1980s – under the watchful eyes of Iain Sinclair's 'style cowboys', not least the editors of *The Penguin Book of Contemporary British Poetry* (1982) – had their own lines to police. 'From Kensal Rise to Heaven' shows this one eyeing the Chinese calendar girl – 'naked, chaste and varnished' – at the local takeaway; noting 'blood trails down the street / from the night before'; observing how the dogs 'vet the garbage before the refuse collectors'; how the pigeons 'inhabit a ruined chiropodist's, coming and going freely / through broken windows into their cosy excremental hollow'. If Hofmann cultivates the frisson of danger, he knows bathos can also be a useful get-out clause.

Hofmann is good at disturbed, mismanaged lives, good at slipping us into Lowell's 'kingdom of the mad'. The opening of 'Against Nature' is spectacular: 'Des Esseintes himself would have admired / her fastidiousness – anorexia, years in hospital – / as he gloated over his own peptone enemas . . .' 'Against Nature' takes us near to that point where writing and cruelty are almost interchangeable (little risk of *la tenerezza* here). Yet the anorexic who 'walks fast to lose weight' is peculiarly ennobled by the poem's details: 'In a gesture of self-betrayal, she goes shopping: / powdered milk, Gitanes, cans of cat food / to placate Sappho, her black panther of a cat . . .' Her judgement of men is woefully poor: a one-time Japanese lodger 'drank as much beer / in an evening as a special Kobe beef cow' and 'He never cleaned the bath, and left rich stains / in the lavatory bowl, like a dirty protest . . .' The boyfriend, 'weird, well-spoken, / Jesus bearded', is 'an anonymous depressive', something 'out of Dostoevsky', who is often denied access.

> Then his notes bristle on the doormat like fakirs,
> her name on them in big block capitals,
> widely spaced on the paranoid envelope . . .

The boyfriend's missives are literary transactions of sorts. Which takes us to 'My Father's House', the second part of

Acrimony, where the poems of hurt and betrayal were so beautifully and un-flinchingly executed one wondered how Hofmann might ever be able to surpass them.

Discussing Robert Lowell's prose in *Behind the Lines*, Hofmann dwells on the American's autobiographical writing, including '91 Revere Street' whose material was refashioned to make several of the poems in *Life Studies*. Lowell on the home front, according to Hofmann, is Lowell at his sardonic best. It is inevitable that one mentions Lowell in the same breath as Hofmann's poems about his father. Philip Larkin's indictment of parenthood seems (as it almost always does) germane. They fuck you up but *how* they fuck you up, and maybe we know even when it's happening there are creative dividends in being fucked up.

From *Nights in the Iron Hotel* through to the elegiac poems in *Approximately Nowhere*, via the first section of *Corona, Corona*, [The] Father's House has borne down on the writing of the son with as much pressure as the poetic of Robert Lowell. The voice of the New England American qualifies the bloodbond of the German father. Lowell (who knew everything one could know about hierarchy) supplied, in large part, the laconic, turbo-driven means by which the 'English' poet could stake out his independence from the German father and engineer '[his] own birth in the new country' ('The Machine That Cried'). Oedipus, it would seem, had more than one passport.

In the foreword to his selection of Lowell (in Faber's Poet-to-Poet series), Hofmann speaks about the 'inexhaustible amplitude' of Lowell's writing which has kept him going back to the American since he first read him as an undergraduate in 1976 (by which time, paradoxically, 'The Age of Lowell' was drawing to a close). It's instructive to observe how often Lowell becomes a point of reference in *Behind the Lines*, a touchstone, a supplier of terms for Hofmann's variegated readings of other

– typically European – writers. A discussion of Montale, for example, quickly dovetails into reflections on Lowell's translations in *Imitations*: 'At this moment I would guess that *Imitations* is more influential than any other aspect of Lowell's poetic practice'; and any discussion of Hofmann's poetic must now accommodate his role as a translator of prose. A reading of Ian Hamilton's 'The Visit' discovers, likewise, something of Lowell's 'Waking in the Blue'. Ian Hamilton, a biographer of Lowell no less, is a poet whose every poem 'is pruned back to an austere and beautiful knot of pain', and Hamilton is a rare English presence in Hofmann's collection of review pieces.

Lowell has left his fingerprints all over Hofmann's poetry. Not only does Hofmann's writing enjoy that laidback, prosy certitude, the very notations of his punctuation – lapidary hyphens, elliptical withdrawal, presence and absence – not to mention the adjectival clusters, the tell-tale triads (and more), all speak of Hofmann's familiarity with the American poet. David Wheatley, in this publication, refers to Adorno's designation of punctuation marks as 'traffic signals'. Hofmann's readers have learnt to pull up, more or less in one piece, in some pleasingly unsalubrious cul-de-sac. The Anglo-German poet gives us a Europeanized version of Lowell's idiomatic drawl (*almost* clumsy), but always knowing exactly when to cut through the fat with surgical speed. Sometimes, too, Lowell's very lines are reworked or co-opted for Hofmann's own purposes. 'And the Teeth of the Children Are Set on Edge', from *Acrimony*, begins 'It's the twenty-fifth and I'm twenty-five', immediately recalling 'These are the tranquillised Fifties, and I am forty' from 'Memories of West Street and Lepke'.

Confessionalism is described as the 'C-word' in Hofmann's Faber introduction to Lowell, and that 'nasty little label' in his piece on Hamilton in *Behind the Lines*. Like Lowell's writing, like Hamilton's, Hofmann's father-son poems have little to do with psychic conflagration, have little to do with 'the poet as psycho-pharmaceutical centrifuge', as Hofmann describes John Berryman in his compelling Faber selection (2004). Lowell's poems about his father in *Life Studies* are cool, melancholic, almost kindly pieces. Hofmann's 'My Father's House', on the basis of title alone, steps away from solipsism, at least for a moment, to suggest a range of Biblical, Freudian and mythical possibilities. Hofmann on Hofmann – the poet-son (not shut up in prose) 'reading' the novelist-father, where poetry thumbs its nose at patriarchal narratives, where the ink is thicker than the blood, where in 'The Means of Production' the father places novels between himself and his pursuers like 'a man pleading for his life' – might be seen as taking its place in a wider set of wider negotiations. 'My Father's House', in this light, might evoke writers as varied as Turgenev, Edmund Gosse and J. M. Synge, whose *The Playboy of the Western World* makes us believe the father has been slain, only to reveal later he is merely wounded. Hofmann's poems transcend their own novelistic precisions – '*Gert Hofmann, travelling in Yugoslavia in a silver Audi 100 . . .*' – to insinuate the wider tragedy of twentieth-century Europe complete with border guards and contested frontiers.

Behind the Lines (dedicated to the memory of Gert Hofmann) enables us to go back to the poetry of Hofmann, a poetry of citations, allusions, German fragments, re-armed with a high-velocity glossary. It's impossible, for example, not to place Hofmann's review of his father's novel *Our Conquest* alongside 'Author, Author', the longest poem in *Acrimony*. The review (also from 1986) is sometimes revealingly hesitant, unlike Hofmann's criticism in general, as if the subject were testing the reviewer. *Our Conquest*, set in Germany in May 1945, during the first twenty-four hours of peace, insinuates its way into the Pyrrhic victories (the silent skirmishes!) of *père* and *fils* as revealed to us in *Acrimony*. 'Author, Author' enmeshes public with private:

To come upon by chance, while emptying the dustbin,
the ripped, glittery foil-wrapping of his heart-medicines,

multiplication times-tables of empty capsules,
dosages like police ammunition in a civil disturbance,

or:

If sex is nostalgia for sex, and food nostalgia for food,
his can't be – what did a child of the War get to eat

that he would want to go on eating, and to share?
Standing in the road as the American trucks rolled by:

chewing-gum, cigarettes, canned herrings, a kick in the
teeth.

and, by the end:

I ask myself what sort of consummation is available?
Fight; talk literature and politics; get drunk together?

Kiss him goodnight, as though half my life had never
happened?

Lowell's influence would have been much less interesting had Hofmann not also looked across the English Channel towards Europe. His 'dispatches from the review front' remind us that Hofmann is not only a poet-translator, he's also a cultural broker dextrously lining up Benn and Montale with Lowell in his Faber introduction to the American poet. We might see a poem like 'Author, Author' as a combination of Lowell's laconicism and that German quality of *Schonungslosigkeit* (unsparingness) which Hofmann recognizes in Otto Dix.

Hofmann's collection of poets, novelists, artists in *Behind the Lines* is made up of mostly Americans of the mid-twentieth century and Germans and Europeans from the earlier modernist period. The line-up is mouth-watering; it includes: Wallace Stevens, John Berryman, Frederick Seidel, Gottfried Benn, Georg Trakl, Bertolt Brecht, Paul Celan, Anna Akhmatova, Joseph Brodsky, Eugenio Montale, Otto Dix, Malcolm Lowry, Paul Bowles, Robert Musil, Joseph Roth, not to mention the Irish trio Heaney, Muldoon and Paulin, whose *Fivemiletown* is treated with such relish.

Behind the Lines is rather like a roll call of Hofmann's 'army of stragglers': prisoners, war-poets, survivors, skulkers, suicides, drug addicts, madmen, exiles, émigrés, fugitives, dissidents and persecuted Jews. (Antecedents in some way, perhaps, of Gert Hofmann's novelistic characters: 'maniacs, compulsive, virtuoso talkers, talkers for dear life, / talkers in soliloquies, notebooks, tape-recordings, last wills . . .') Ironically, Gert Hofmann says in the BBC documentary: 'I am not a poetic person. I like tense situations, I like people colliding and telling each other unpleasant truths which has nothing to do with poetry'(!). Georg Trakl, who threatened to kill himself when a sweet-shop owner refused him credit and who then did so after the battle of Grodek in 1914, seems the kind of 'German' poet Michael Hofmann would seize upon. Hofmann's description of Trakl – the 'quiet, monotonous voice, and the evil, metallic, criminal glitter of his eyes' – eclipses Donald Davie's 'reek of the human' because it hints at the weird glamour of the pathological.

The book reviewing got off the ground when Hofmann's first poems began to appear (1980). Hofmann, in fact, almost as a matter of course, blurs the distinction between criticism and poetry. His poetry typically *is* a form of literary criticism. The critical pieces are, like the poems, full of dazzling surfaces and aphoristic fiat. Of Ian Hamilton's narrow poetic focus, his wife's mental illness and the death of the father by cancer,

Hofmann concludes that such poetry 'is not craftsmanship or profession, but catastrophe'. To which he adds: 'I can't, in general terms, think of any better way for a poem to be.' And at moments there's no shortage of animus. *A Book of Memories*, by Péter Nádas, we are told, for example, 'must have been grindingly unpleasant to translate'. The reviews are performances in their own right – aleatory, stylish, sometimes necessarily brutal. What better than to finish with Gottfried Benn, that unabashed aesthete, who argued: 'You can learn tight-rope walking, funambulism, high-wire acts, walking on nails, but a fascinating way with words, you either have it or you don't.'

Saying What Happened:
Michael Hofmann and Confessional Poetry

DENNIS O'DRISCOLL

When I hear the words 'confessional poetry', I reach for my Anne Sexton, for poems like 'The Ballad of the Lonely Masturbator', or 'For My Lover, Returning to His Wife'. Or I think of Sharon Olds at her most invasive: 'Hitler entered Paris the way my / sister entered my room at night, / sat astride me, squeezed me with her knees, / held her thumbnails to the skin of my wrists and / peed on me . . .'. Or I revisit the collected editions – solid as the four Mount Rushmore sculptures – of the founding fathers and mother: Sylvia Plath, Robert Lowell, W. D. Snodgrass, John Berryman. Not that the latter would have welcomed so reductive a tag, as this brusque exchange, from his *Paris Review* interview with Peter Stitt, makes clear – and loud:

> INTERVIEWER: You, along with Lowell, Sylvia Plath, and several others, have been called a confessional poet. How do you react to that label?
> BERRYMAN: With rage and contempt! Next question.
> INTERVIEWER: Are the sonnets 'confessional'?
> BERRYMAN: Well, they're about her and me. I don't know. The word doesn't mean anything. I understand the confessional to be a place where you go and talk with a priest. I personally haven't been to confession since I was twelve years old.

W. D. Snodgrass reacted no less jumpily: 'I never cared for the term *confessional* in the least. Without any disrespect to M. L. Rosenthal, I think it's a journalistic tag, not very accurate. It sounds either like you're some kind of religious poet, which I am not, or as if you write bedroom memoirs, and I hope I don't come under that heading . . . My poems were called confessional because I wrote about the facts of my own life, and particularly about losing a daughter in a divorce'.

The M. L. Rosenthal reference is, of course, to the American critic whose book *The New Poets* (1967) labelled and packaged the 'confessional' school, launching the term into the mainstream discussion of poetry: 'Because of the way Lowell brought his private humiliations, sufferings and psychological problems into the poems of *Life Studies*, the word "confessional" seemed appropriate enough.' Rosenthal's inventory of Lowell characteristics also serves as a checklist of some defining attributes of Michael Hofmann's poetry: poems that place 'the literal Self' at 'the center of the poem', and yet are 'more than merely a self-analytical case history'; poems that are saturated with 'a sense of objective reality', that echo 'the actual speech of his family and their friends', and show 'condescension and contempt' – tempered with compassion – for the poet's father.

Moreover, Rosenthal, summarizing Lowell's confessional 'phase', set out the challenge facing any aspiring successor – a role for which Michael Hofmann has proved to be the most eligible candidate of recent decades, meeting every requirement of the job with aplomb: 'confessional' poetry was 'an impermanent but indispensable phase of Lowell's development, but indicates as well that only a comparable deployment of energies and resources would justify another poet's trying the same thing. Nothing could be more sterile and obviously self-deceptive than the use of a "confessional" mannerism in a trivial or immature way. In other words, the method is so demanding, and must be so idiosyncratic in its execution, that its seductiveness may well turn out to be disastrous to others who lack Lowell's very great strengths.'

Hofmann's indebtedness to Robert Lowell was confessed from the start. Reviewing his *Collected Poems*, he began at the beginning: 'It was reading Robert Lowell that brought me to poetry at the age of 19, in 1976 . . . I find his poems endlessly approachable, wonderfully communicative and perfectly inexhaustible: stately, supple, personal and resourceful.' He is certainly justified in asserting that there is a great deal more to Lowell's poetry than the 'confessional' tag suggests, and that his 'artful poems . . . mock such an appellation': 'This fails to take account of anything done in language: it treats all language as equal and irrelevant.' Nonetheless, confessional elements form an essential component of the Lowell mix, and Hofmann is less than convincing when he underplays them: 'The degree to which [Lowell's poems] presume on the reader's human involvement with their subject matter is negligible. They do not serve prurience by dishing up a stream of private and discreditable things.' Elizabeth Hardwick's heartfelt objection to the incorporation of her letters in *The Dolphin* lies muffled behind this remark, as does the scolding sigh of the other Elizabeth at the centre of Lowell's life, Miss Bishop, 'Art *just isn't worth that much.*'

The notion of 'confession', as generally understood in the phrase 'confessional poetry', implies the airing by the poet of transgressive or confidential material of a personal nature, normally interdicted on grounds of decorum, sensitivity or confidentiality. It transposes the church pew with the Freudian couch; as the sacrament of confession confers spiritual healing on the contrite, psychoanalysis administers a talking cure to the 'analysand'. Flying in the face of − indeed reacting against − T. S. Eliot's doctrine of poetry as an 'escape from personality' rather than 'an expression of personality', confessional poetry wallows in personal material. In an age that places unprecedented emphasis both on self-fulfilment and on victimhood, it enables poetry practitioners to gratify their well-developed capacity for self-absorption. Sharon Olds declares of her mother, 'Like many of us, she's not interested in much except herself'. And not only are confessional poets licensed to focus on their favourite topic – themselves – but the self-styled 'victims' among them can spread (and thus shed) their inner poisons in public and, like lurid daytime chatshow guests, place a premium on shock value.

'When I'm writing a poem of mine', Olds remarks, 'it's not as if anyone's forced to read it . . . If they find themselves in some presence that is unappealing to them, they will just close the book, put the magazine down, throw it across the room! I trust everyone to protect themselves – if shock is a bad thing. I love being shocked by people's poems.' In practice, many confessional poets lean lightly on the shock tactics, having nothing more startling to fess to than single parenthood, skid-row upbringing, skirmishes with alcohol or cocaine; others proudly parade their adulteries: little life stories rounded with a bland epiphanic rally, a token verbal orgasm, at poem's end. But, like all poetic genres, confessionalism has enormous potential in accomplished hands. 'Who the hell cares about Anne Sexton's grandmother?' W. H. Auden supposedly spluttered after a poetry reading. The poet must make us care, beguile us into caring; invest more skill in the telling than the tale and, paradoxically, exemplify a self-forgetful confessionalism. This course is comprehensively plotted by Joan Aleshire in her vigorous 'defense of the lyric':

> Shakespeare in the sonnets, Keats, and Yeats speak from the self's particular viewpoint, but for these poets, it's not only life's experience that interests, but how what has been thought and felt – the burden seeking release – can be made into the experience of a poem. The act of making the poem as a piece of work outside the self draws the poet's attention away from the self and into the work, which makes its own commands. True concentration on craft is an act of forgetting the self.
>
> In the confessional poem, as I'd like to define it, the poet, overwhelmed or intoxicated by the facts of his or

her life, lets the facts take over. To say that a poem is confessional is to signal a breakdown in judgement and craft . . . I see the confessional poem as a plea for special treatment, a poem where the poet's stance is one of particularity apart from common experience. Confession in art, as in life, can be self-serving – an attempt to shift the burden of knowledge from speaker-transgressor to listener.

No contemporary poet, and certainly no poet of his generation, has employed the confessional mode with greater flair, éclat, originality and control than Michael Hofmann. He has reshaped and reimagined this overheated genre, lending it a new lease of life by counter-intuitively shifting its focus from calculated sensation and shameless self-revelation to a vehicle for dispassionate truth: a tool as sharp, cool and unforgiving as a scalpel blade. In this, he brings to mind the self-portraits of Lucian Freud, another German-born artist domiciled in England: works in which spirit is made flesh and the self is painted objectively – indeed, as mere object. The artist beholds himself not through the mirror of Narcissus but through the cold eye of a coroner's lens, neither donning a mask nor adopting a persona.

The 'I' of a Hofmann poem is as detached and impersonal as the 'he' of J. M. Coetzee's chilling memoirs, *Boyhood* and *Youth*; interest in the self arises from bafflement rather than entrancement. To charge Hofmann's work with narcissism ('I stare at myself in the grey, oxidized mirror') would be to overlook the fact that the poet is mystified, not enthralled, by himself. He writes to prove to himself that he actually exists; the parade of uppercase 'I's in the poetry is that of a disinterested witness, not an egotist. 'Do you think I'm real?', a lover asks him in 'Lewis Hollow Road'; he implicitly directs the same question at himself, and his sense of self is too tentative for egotism to take root. Besides – as Michael Hamburger, also an Anglo-German poet-translator, observed – even where, 'outside his poems', a poet *is* an egotist, 'inside them he feels his ego dissolve, intermingle with all that he names or invokes'. Master of the 'list' poem, Hofmann is an inveterate namer and invoker.

He resolved, from the start, that his poetry should be 'as truthful as I can make it': 'If you want to make something up, you write a novel.' For Hofmann, the poet's burden of proof is of a different order to the novelist's. Prolific translator of novels though he is, his scepticism regarding novelists' notion of 'truth' was graphically displayed in the BBC film about father and son screened in 1990, in which he expressed his determination to establish 'the truth about my father's life': 'I don't want to hear about any more fictional figures.' Discussing *The Film Explainer* – a novel by Hofmann *père*, translated by Hofmann *fils* – in which the life of Gert's grandfather is purportedly charted, the poet cross-examined his father on (rather than *in*) camera. He became increasingly impatient at what he sensed to be Gert's evasions about the background to that novel, despite the novelist's exasperated insistence that the grandfather is 'not an invented person at all': 'Is he a real person?'; 'Was he your real grandfather?'; 'He was your physical grandfather, called Karl Hofmann?'; 'I might have believed you if you had told me about him when I was three, instead of thirty-three. You have now had thirty years in which to make him up.' The duplicity evident in Gert's own life ('Two routes in his head, two itineraries, two women') does nothing to enhance his credibility.

Writing which is both truthful and deeply personal will incline, to a greater or lesser extent, toward the confessional – whether with the teasing subtlety of Shakespeare's sonnets or the amatory passion and pain that unfold, like a costume drama, in the Renaissance-spirited *Berryman's Sonnets* – twenty-one of which Hofmann included in his Berryman selection for Faber's Poet-to-Poet series. 'When Shakespeare wrote, "Two loves I have", reader, he was *not kidding*', Berryman insisted. Having endured Michael's persistent surveillance, Gert Hofmann was offended by the resultant poems – poems of which the novelist was the icily-observed subject. The extent of his disapproval and his hurt was evident when, after a reading by the novelist in September 1985, I asked him about the poems (by then disseminated widely in literary magazines) that would soon be gathered in *Acrimony* (1986), his son's second, and finest, collection. Suffice it to say, I am in no doubt as to the appropriateness of the book's title.

Michael's vow to tell the truth, the whole truth, was encapsulated in an interview by Paul Bailey. Invited by the latter to instance some 'particularly un-English quality' embodied by his work, he immediately cited 'candour'; in continental Europe, he added, the assumption that certain subjects are taboo would be 'rather shocking'. Alert to the un-English forthrightness of *Acrimony*, Blake Morrison, having characterized the collection as 'a very confessional book', wrote, 'It is hard to imagine any English son writing with such unkind candour about his begetter, especially when that begetter is a public figure'.

Hofmann's pledges of full disclosure bear their most tart fruit in the 'My Father's House' section of *Acrimony*, where the elder Hofmann's less endearing features ('salami breath', 'forced bonhomie', infidelity), are paraded with warts-and-all inclusiveness ('We are as the warts on your elbows'). 'Bad-tempered and irritable', a bone-gnawing, domineering paterfamilias, Gert has 'gone to seed like Third World dictators, / fat heads of state suffering horribly / from Western diseases whose name is Legion'; and he has lived the lie of a 'double life' for years – a contentious, provocative character reference for a father, still very much alive at the time, to gnaw on.

Prevalent though Hofmann's confessional traits undoubtedly are (not least in the reaction shots of himself that feature in his family scenes), they are, like Lowell's confessions, an inevitable consequence, an occupational hazard, of unflinching scrutiny of self and others. He does not set out to *épater la bourgeoisie* – or any other class or group. W. H. Auden's definition of poetry as 'the clear expression of mixed feelings' is vividly exemplified by the father-son poems: eidetic, photorealistic recollections that are by no means devoid of flashes of affection, notably when summoning a period in which the young Michael looked up to his father and yearned to 'share' his life ('I had a worshipful proximity with him, / companionable and idolatrous'). After his father's death, their life-share is complete: 'I physically felt myself become him. I felt something within me which I felt was him, and I was very happy to have it there. So, he's no longer outside me or beside me or above me to be taken issue with.'

Louise Glück's trenchant essay 'The Forbidden' includes a deadly critique of Linda McCarriston's book *Eva-May*, anatomising the reader's conflicted relationship with works that are harrowing in subject matter, yet oddly vainglorious in manner: 'The test for emotional authority is emotional impact, and the great flaw in Linda McCarriston's *Eva-May* is that, cumulatively, it isn't moving. And it is meant to be read this way, as a whole, as it is most certainly intended to move, to shock, to break the heart. One feels in these poems the delight of the ambitious artist at discovering terrain this promising: how could anything as powerful as incest fail to make devastating art?' All artists in the grip of fertile subject matter, however sombre or tragic, will evince some irrepressible glee at its rich creative potential. No more fallow periods. No more scratching around for stimulation. They are up and running. Michael Hofmann is no exception: 'Until I found my father . . . I didn't have anything continuous to relate, a big subject, or a place where things cohered.' But unlike the poetry of victimhood, in which the *dramatis personae* are assigned clear-cut, non-negotiable roles as goodies or baddies, victims and perpetrators, Michael Hofmann's concern is not with victimhood or blame. As unsparing of himself as of others, his determination to follow the truth, wherever it may lead, lends his poems their edginess and adventurousness, urgency and unpredictability; emotional preoccupations are never allowed to overwhelm literary principles.

Dense, intense, brisk and gnarled – crackling with macaronic coinages and dry asides – his poems seldom waste a word; even the most casual-seeming utterance proves its worth. Prosy, plain and verbose by comparison, Sharon Olds's collection, *The Father* (1992), is dominated by news bulletins from the battle zone of the cancer ward: 'He looked like / someone killed in a bloodless struggle – / the strain in his neck and the base of his head, / as if he were violently pulling back.' The book is by no means without merit; 'The Race', its outstanding poem (a breathless sprint to catch her father's last breath), is a poignant masterwork. But some of the father poems spill over – in a mess of mucus, blood, sperm and phlegm – into the realms of the voyeuristic and transgressive. Fascinated by body parts and body functions, she takes a naughty, guilt-salted pleasure in the shameless and tasteless ('I want / to be in him, as I was once inside him, / riding in his balls the day before he cast me'). Skin-deep truths are of scant interest to Hofmann.

Between the early poems in which Gert Hofmann is scrutinized and the later ones where he is elegized, are the biographical thumbnails, marked by Lowell's *Life Studies* and *History,* which open *Corona, Corona* (1993), Michael Hofmann's third collection. Among the father-son relationships depicted there, the more lethal ones include a son-killing father (Marvin Gaye's) and a father-slaying son (the aptly-named artist, Richard Dadd). Although the Gert-Michael conflict is non-violent – a war of words, a clash of genres, between poet and novelist – *Corona, Corona* confirms Michael's ongoing obsession with father-son tensions. His paternal accounting reaches an interim reckoning in his fourth collection, *Approximately Nowhere* (1999), where he comes not to bury or to praise Gert (who died in 1993) but to remember him exactly as he perceived him. Neither confession

nor absolution is much in evidence; again, the impulse is towards truth-telling. In one nimble line-break, he writes of his
father's 'tenderness' – wait for it! – 'for a firefly'. The son has had
the last word; but the *Approximately Nowhere* poems are unlikely
to be his last words about his father:

> Last words? Probably not, or none that I knew of,
> by the sea with your grandsons in another country
> when it happened. A completed manuscript on your desk,
>
> and some months before, a choleric note dashed off to me
> cutting me off, it would once have been said,
> for nothing I could this time see that I'd done wrong . . .

'What Happens' in *Approximately Nowhere* alludes to Robert
Lowell's poem 'Epilogue' ('why not say what happened?'). To
relate what happened, Hofmann asserts somewhat defensively
in a Poetry Book Society note, is not the same as being 'confessional':

> The poem may not get written without its hurt or its
> drama, but it's not the hurt or the drama that make it
> a poem. Those things are, literally and punningly, a
> 'pretext' . . . A 'confessional poem' is a contradiction in
> terms; the action is by definition elsewhere. The reader,
> quite properly, responds to it exactly as he would to a
> piece of news or gossip: 'Lovely for you!' or 'Oh, you
> poor thing!' And that's why he's perhaps a little mul-
> ish when it's put to him that he might read such a poem
> – Olds or Sexton or lesser Berryman, to name some
> names, *again*. Why should he, he's heard it before . . .

Confessional tendencies, such as they are, in *Approximately
Nowhere* manifest themselves mostly in the libidinal domain,

where the kissing-and-telling relates to infidelity. The bluntly-titled 'Fucking' recalls 'our extravagant happiness, / matched or cancelled / by the equal and opposite unhappiness of others' and 'our last, stolen day for a month'. In the book's final poem, 'balls' are flashed more ironically than in Olds's poem, though no less outrageously. Without the example of Robert Lowell in his confessional moods, Hofmann might well have become a less various, even more incorrigibly bookish, poet than he proved to be. But some dirty linen is best left unwashed and unconfessed:

> You sleep in a nest of my dirty shirts,
> while, five or six time zones adrift of you
> and in temperatures close to blood heat, I keep my balls
> coddled in your second-best lace panties
> for the duration.

King-Wilkinson

HUGO WILLIAMS

Tiny, old, completely bald,
yet strangely recognisable still
in his winter plumage – no,
not myself this time,
caught sight of in a mirror,
making me jump out of my skin,

but an old school friend
whose hand I used to hold,
advancing towards me across the room,
as across the years, saying:
'You remember me, don't you?
I used to be King-Wilkinson.'

Whatever

RANDALL MANN

1

So, Michael Hofmann: wild-eyed, charmingly dishevelled, twitchy, threatening-to-be-handsome Michael, who taught my graduate poetry workshop at the University of Florida in the spring of 1996; who made smoking look like the thing one did, naturally, rather than the thing one should think about not doing; who made me feel good about my pack-a-day Salem Lights habit.

2

About a month before that workshop started, Michael had published a review of Donald Justice's *New and Selected Poems* in the *New York Times Book Review*, where he basically called Justice, as I recall, a dusty, fussy relic of fifties formalism. The main problem, if that's the word, was that Michael was hired because of the vacancy left by Justice, who had taught at Florida for ten years, a towering poetry presence on campus. At the time I thought the exercise a little unfortunate and tacky, I who had read Justice off the page and counted a handful of Justice poems as the things most important; a few of my peers shared my thoughts. We grumbled. We plotted against Michael over coffee, at the keg. Against him from the jump.

3

And then there was the workshop when he brought in poems by Lavinia Greenlaw, his then partner, poems from her book *Night Photograph*. It didn't matter, of course, that these poems were delicate and thoughtful and beautifully accomplished, especially for a first collection. No. How dare he make such a rookie mistake, showing us poems of his girl and expecting us to admire them. (And when I met her, she was lovely, which was worse.) We were savage and petty.

4

In class, we read the long poems of Anthony Hecht. Hecht, who had just responded to that Justice review – a 'querulous, dismissive review,' Hecht wrote in the *New York Times* – which now looks a little small, the response I mean. Michael taught 'The Short End' and 'The Venetian Vespers', poems I had read but not really *read*, with passion and grace and humility. Never mind the poet. I liked that.

5

I loved Michael's brilliant talk but his written criticism on our poems was, how shall I say this, austere and a bit off-to-the-side. (The poet Geri Doran, who also studied with Michael, told me about the time that she once looked very closely at the small scrawl next to one of her lines – only to discover that her line reminded him, apropos of nothing, of a flower.) And yet. One week I turned in a poem about, okay, bathroom sex; I wanted to describe the four urinals, and I wrote that they were 'like boats', but something was missing, and what was that? 'Like boats upended,' he scrawled. Of course. *Upended.*

6

That spring I was inclined to dismiss things dramatically in class by holding up one hand, palm facing out, and wryly, wearingly proclaiming, 'Whatever.' A couple years later, in his book *Approximately Nowhere*, Michael published the great poem 'Summer', with these ending lines: 'The sky between leaves is the brightest thing in nature, / Virginia Woolf told the inquiring Rupert Brooke. Whatever.' When I read this I laughed and kicked myself for being all talk and not this clever and flattered myself to think he had stolen this gesture from me. Ha.

7

Each workshop was essentially a warm-up for the Market Street Bar, where we almost always ended up. Thank god for booze, it made things with Michael less awkward. Michael eyed our well drinks and cheap beer warily and ordered a Pilsner Urquell. He fidgeted and stared bleakly into his beer. I told him that here in the South, since he was fifteen years older than I, he could be my father! I had lost track of how many drinks. Michael stayed, inscrutable. I excused myself for a smoke.

8

For a time, he and I lived in the same apartment complex, Arlington Square – the setting of one of his best poems 'Freebird' – 'a blue by pink downtown development'. He was 'cuntstruck and fat', or he was in that poem; I was cock-hungry and thin, my diet of gin and fags and pills and poems. Some early mornings, which is to say the butt-ends of the night, it was just me and the pool shark, in the pool on the blue side, where Michael lived.

9

One day, we must have been talking about Robert Lowell (Michael talked a lot about Lowell), which led us to Ian Hamilton, Lowell's biographer. Have you read his poems, he asked. I hadn't, and he was so convinced of my need for Hamilton that he bought me the book himself. Well, it was something else, the sheer economy of Hamilton's poems, these ingenious miniatures, 'Memorial' and 'The Recruits' and 'Metaphor' and 'Midwinter' and 'Complaint' and 'Home' ('The ice / That catches in your hair melts on my tongue') and 'Critique' and on and on. This love of Hamilton he shared is an un-repayable gift.

'The Hysterical Use of the Present Tense'

DECLAN RYAN

In his biography of Robert Lowell, Ian Hamilton noted that, after abandoning his Brahmin-baiting Catholicism, Lowell had faith only in 'the imaginable moral power of perfect speech'. 'Perfect' may seem an odd term to use about Lowell, a poet who went on to publish so prolifically, in relatively unperfected collections such as *Notebook*, but the notion of 'perfect speech' is one which was crucial to Hamilton and, via both his and Lowell's influence, one to which a number of the poems in *Approximately Nowhere* might lay claim. 'Perfection' is, typically, a little more complicated than it may first appear – this Hamiltonian coinage isn't one of his famously exacting measures of quality, but rather a semi-mystical mode of lyric poetry by which a poet can, if he gets it right, raise the dead.

In Hamilton's preface to his own *Fifty Poems* he sheds a little more light on what he meant by 'perfect speech', writing 'But did I truly think that poetry, if perfect, could bring back the dead? In some ways yes, I think I did.' So how did Hamilton believe one might go about resurrecting the dead armed with just 'a few melancholy poems', as he puts it in 'Epitaph'? The key for Hamilton was to tap into a platonic realm of discourse with the speaking voice, one which almost always found itself addressing a 'you' who isn't the reader, but rather, as he put it when in conversation with Dan Jacobson:

> someone who couldn't answer back. Although the poem created the illusion of an address, it's the sort of address you might make over someone's grave . . .
> The poems are ideal speech, what one would like to say

to the addressees – if they were alive or were capable of attending·

Hamilton's output is littered with poems addressed to his late father, where Hamilton Snr is the aforementioned 'you' and, to revisit 'Epitaph', 'If I had touched you then / One of us might have survived.' For Hamilton, a 'poem of perfection' required suffering, but crucially that suffering couldn't be his own, rather it had to belong to the 'you' being addressed. His poems became, then, a heady mixture of *esprit de l'escalier*, prolonged apology and magic; an unusual blend for such a hard-nosed critic perhaps, but one which was crucial if the poems were to serve their one true function, which Hamilton outlined in an interview with Peter Dale:

> One knew that in life ordinary speech made little difference, couldn't save the other person from death or from illness. Poetic speech might work differently. Some magic seemed to be required. While writing a poem, one could have the illusion that one was talking in a magic way to the subject of the poem. One might even think that this is doing some good, making things better. And then, of course, you know it isn't. You wake up and find it hasn't.

Crucially, in order for his 'perfect speech' to work, to have a chance of 'doing some good', it had to occur in the present tense, because to relive it in this way, to create a 'you' who may be incapable of attending in ordinary life but who was present as an addressee in a poem, meant that by hitting on the perfect formulation of words perhaps the poet really could salvage the situation, mitigate the suffering, even restore 'you' to life.

In *Approximately Nowhere*, we find another father now incapable of attending. The father once so vivid in *Acrimony* and elsewhere, 'who all my life had been a volcano', has died, as we learn in the book's first new poem, after 1979's poignant (and somewhat Hamiltonian) 'Tea For My Father'. 'For Gert Hofmann, died 1 July 1993' doesn't address anyone, there is no 'you', but the 'action' does occur in the present tense which seems, in its own way, rather shocking. The picture we are given is of a room which has been in a state of decay for some time, needing only death – which has now arrived – to authenticate its sense of loss and stasis. It is a room where Hofmann Snr has been living a cut-off existence, where a rare window on the world, 'the everlasting radio', 'pinked his eye once', and 'The same books as for years, the only additions by himself' seem to confirm this splendid isolation, all watched over by 'an African mask . . . to keep out evil spirits'. If we needed further confirmation that this has been a death scene awaiting its inevitable consummation, it comes at the end of the poem, with the 'berries / on the mountain ash already orange and reddening, although / the inscrutable blackbirds will scorn them months more.' Gert Hofmann, like those berries, we feel, may have been lent time which perhaps he didn't require or demand – there is a sense of his being a character who, like Lowell's mother in *Life Studies*, has mistakenly stayed on a train beyond his required destination.

In 'Last Walk' we witness a subtle, humanising shift when the poet embraces some of Hamilton's other 'perfect speech' techniques to sit alongside it, namely the address of a 'you'. The 'you' in this poem isn't just the late father, it's a plural, parental unit, but because of it the man who had been a mere berry ripe for death's picking becomes part of a mobile duo, one who is no longer merely battening down the hatches but rather strolling 'arm in arm' with his wife of thirty-seven years, and 'stable'. The mood is not dissimilar to 'For Gert Hofmann', with a long-understudied old age now having arrived, the telling presence of an '*alteingesessen*' farm among a new suburb filled with gardens, the advent of a new age, in the shape of an airport 'racing day and night to completion like a new book'. The father – one half of the active, experiencing couple who form the 'you' being addressed – is no longer merely a leftover relic owed 'an odd stone or metal' for his marriage's longevity. Now he is capable of demonstrating 'tenderness for a firefly'. By using the present-tense as recollection method, and the direct address, 'Last Walk' becomes at once confessional and epistolary, capable of incorporating the minutiae of intimate life without their coming across as mere remembrance. The implication of the present tense is that, with their son still making his filial electron-buzzes between them, this tenderness is in some sense ongoing; what does survive is love (of fireflies, in this case).

'Endstation, Erding', in part a companion piece to 'Last Walk', is similarly concerned with the relationship between a remembrance of what has gone and the extent to which it can remain a present tense activity. If 'Last Walk' allows the parents to remain walking, for their arm-in-arm perambulations to exist in a continuous present, 'Endstation, Erding' is concerned with 'the walk the other way', immediately plunging us into something seemingly more final, away from the present and into notions of inheritance. The shift from a past-tense evocation of Gert shopping, picking up 'economies now, bargains' in which he 'took the same pleasure', becomes something more radical towards the poem's close. The poet and his subject elide, without warning. We have no indication that it is anyone other than the bargain-hunting Gert making 'The walk through the deserted postmodern forum / of cobbles and fountains' until we are pulled up short by the library, its 'card *In Gedenken an Gert Hofmann*', and a final line drawing us back again to the opening poem, to Lowell, and to a haunted understanding of the lingering presence of the father in the world; 'the railway signals still up with the line long gone'. Just as this shows how his bruised, banana-buying self endures in his environment, performing a gentle sort of haunting, it also implies that, as in 'For Gert Hofmann', he has to an extent been living in a world which has already memorialized him. Finally, it is also suggestive of the poet's own fate, not only when surrounded by the shades of his father in the general store and postmodern forum, but also destined to some day make this same walk 'the other way'.

Inheritance is at the heart of 'Epithanaton' too. Explicitly, in its opening, with the 'choleric note dashed off to me / cutting me off' but also in a more inverted sense, where the children of the deceased attempt a sort of anti-bequest:

> We wanted to bring you things, give you things,
> leave you things – to go with you in some form, I
>   suppose.
> A plastic ivory elephant from my sister,
>
> who mussed up your hair every time they drove a part
>   through it,
> a few crumbs of lavender from me. All of it removed.

Apart from the failure to 'give you things', the most striking element of this passage is once more that 'you'. The direct address is past here, not present, and its impact and implications perhaps best experienced in contrast to the present-tense counterparts in Hamilton's oeuvre. Where the narrator here 'Hardly dared touch you / Your empty open hands on the awful mendacious coverlet, / the ochre bodystocking pancake colour of you' there are numerous examples in Hamilton's bedside vigil poems where similar fears and rituals are played out in the present, the father still alive and, for the duration of the poem at least, 'capable of attending'

> Your shadows blossom now about your bed
> Discolouring
> The last irritated facts.

Your oriental dressing-gown;
Its golden butterflies, laced to their silken leaves,
Ache from the sudden darkness at your door.

('Metaphor')

Your fingers, wisps of blanket hair
Caught in their nails, extend to touch
The bedside roses flaking in the heat.
White petals fall.

('Father, Dying')

The upshot in 'Epithanaton' is that this is not relived, so much
as recalled, despite the direct address, and as much as there is a
sense of haunting in the poem – the Hardy-ish 'You were well-
nigh inaccessible', the adjective '*deadish*' pilfered from the beer
lexicon and doing a lot of work in explaining this there-but-
not-there presence – this is a different sort of epitaph. While
Hamilton's bedside vigils are ongoing, conjured up again in the
act of being written, the one we find in 'Epithanaton' is over and
done with, the 'you' who is being addressed is not to be found
here at least, although it is clear that '*Lebwohl*' is the wrong
word. This picture, the inert, bodystocking-coloured, inaccessible father, is unquestionably one of finality, but the manner
of address, coupled with the poem's conclusion that farewell is
'the inappropriate expression', that the narrator is 'prematurely,
unconscionably, leaving you behind', and the lingering '*dicke
Luft*' all bring us back to the poem's opening line: 'Last words?
Probably not', making us read them in a new light. The fact that
there is still a 'you', added to the present tense of 'Last Walk',
suggests complication, the possibility that more than 'one of us
might have survived' in some sense, that although in this scene
the father is dead, he is in a wider sense only '*deadish*'.

The sense of lingering, which has been a constant thread
throughout the opening poems, is elaborated on in the poems

that follow. 'Zirbelstraße' and the suggestively titled 'Still Life' add a Mr Bleaney-ish air to this atmosphere of past accumulation and clutter gone to seed, building on 'For Gert Hofmann''s 'onetime pond' 'packed with nettles' additional proof 'That how we live measures our own nature'. In 'Zirbelstraße', a moving-out inventory becomes a list of a life, where 'démodé gadgets' and other 'doubtful assets of a lifetime' are packed away, almost ceremonially, just as both the father's mischief and lightning, and the 'high pines that gave the street its name', are cut down. If there isn't a direct address or any other nod towards 'perfect speech', we are nonetheless left in no doubt that the poet is re-living this home-life, that it is just as much a scene of haunting and return as the other domestic poems of loss, as the final lines demonstrate:

> my off-and-on kingdom in the cellar, among the skis
> and old boots,
> my father's author copies and foreign editions,
> the blastproof metal doors, preserves, tin-cans and
> board-games
> of people who couldn't forget the Russians, the furnace
> room
> where my jeans were baked hard against an early
> departure.

'Blastproof', 'preserves' and the 'jeans baked hard against an early departure' all tell their own story of what it is like to be haunted by a family home, and the 'people who couldn't forget the Russians' itself must surely include the narrator who, in 'Epithanaton', looked at his father and saw him as 'Russian, bearded'.

'Still Life' is, as its title suggests, another poem of stasis, the narrator combining that epitome of big-screen inertia, '*La Grande Bouffe*', with 'gathered dust' and the religious overtones of '*in saecula saeculorum*'. In dialogue with 'For Gert Hofmann' and the cellar of 'Zirbelstraße', this is one of a group of poems that pivot around atrophy, and which engage in a tussle with the poems of the present tense, and direct address, indicative of something other than recollection or entrapment and pointing instead to the possibility of continuation, a legacy and inheritance which is alive and which allows the possibility of 'the hysterical use of the present tense', as coined in 'What Happens'. In contrast to 'Still Life''s '*in saecula saeculorum*', in 'Cheltenham' we find 'The days brutally short', and just as we know that '*Lebwohl*' is not the right word, we find that a visit to the graveyard is a present-tense activity in 'Directions'. The 'onetime pond packed with nettles' of 'For Gert Hofmann' is swapped here for 'huge carp in the ponds' and the only 'slabs' are made of cake.

This wrestling between tenses, between direct address and stasis, presence and inaccessibility, is renewed in the final poem of the sequence, 'Metempsychosis'. The battle between elements of 'perfect speech' and their ability to conjure a presence in the 'you' who is 'capable of attending', capable of displaying tenderness or imparting lessons about being a '*homme de peuple*', are seemingly resolved here. The past-tense bedside vigil of 'Epithanaton' differs from Hamilton's filial watches, already aware that whatever 'you' might remain in the poems, or in the air, isn't to be found by the deathbed or at the funeral. Similarly, this transcendent poem begins with an acceptance that 'Your race [is] run' before building to a climax where 'the ants queened themselves . . . Got to the end.' For a sequence about a father, about death and inheritance, it is fascinating to witness the ways in which the poet takes what he needs from two of his own poetic 'fathers', Lowell and Hamilton, borrowing some of their faith in 'the imaginable moral power of perfect speech', their talking cures and Freudian concerns, but adapting them to suit his own experience of 'leaving you behind', only finding himself able to buy into some of their 'beliefs'. At the end, with his flowers 'blue for faith', he can assert both that 'overbearing children play, / . . . itching / to tear down the bookshelves and inherit the earth' and that 'The clever ones / would go far, to be in position for / the next pedestrian incarnation.'

The Hazards of Travelling

HANS MAGNUS ENZENSBERGER

White spots on the map,
adventure, *Endurance*, discovery –
those were the days!

As to ourselves, all we risk
are body searches
corralled in airports, boredom
and traffic jams on Mount Everest.
Woe betide the luxury cruise,
the backpacker's hostel
and the manager's desperate training
for survival on desolate islands.

When locusts and termites reach
their most destructive growth phase,
biologists speak of the *swarming stage*.
Observers of venture capital will agree.

Better, perhaps, to launch an expedition,
twenty minutes by underground
and a short walk into a *terrain vague*
of backwaters and deserted Victorian mills
leading up to a forgotten cemetery.
Overgrown gravel paths,
wild dog-roses, frost-bitten angels,
weathered tombstones, bygone names
difficult to decipher.

A voyage into our only remaining
dark continent: the past.

Michael Hofmann's London

MARK FORD

Places, and place names, play a major role in the poetry of Michael Hofmann. Reading his work I am sometimes put in mind of one of Wallace Stevens's Adagia: 'Life is an affair of people not of places. But for me life is an affair of places and that is just the trouble.' Title after title introduces us to a poem set in a particular place: 'In Connemara', 'Myopia in Rupert Brooke Country', 'From Kensal Rise to Heaven', 'Avenue A', 'On the Beach at Thorpeness', 'Postcard from Cuernavaca', 'Calle 12 Septiembre', 'Sunday in Puebla', 'Guanajuato Two Times', 'Endstation, Erding', 'Cheltenham', 'Essex', 'Hotel New York, Rotterdam', 'Near Hunstanton', 'Malvern Road', 'Lewis Hollow Road' . . . And many lines of many other poems are taken up by poetic description of place, often to the point that the act of description itself becomes the poem's motor or narrative.

The documentary impulse has always been strong in Hofmann's poetry. It is nearly always melded, however, as it frequently is in, say, the poetry of Robert Lowell, with an expressionist theatricality that shapes the process of description into an oblique, or not so oblique, self-portrait. We come to know Hofmann, or at least come to feel we know his poetic persona, through the way he describes the places he finds himself in.

I want to focus in particular on Hofmann's descriptions of London. An anthology I recently edited, *London: A History in Verse* (2012), includes three of Hofmann's London poems, one from each of his last three books (there are no specifically London poems in his first, *Nights in the Iron Hotel*). I selected 'From Kensal Rise to Heaven' from *Acrimony*, 'From A to B and Back

Again' from *Corona, Corona*, and 'Malvern Road' from *Approximately Nowhere*. Had I had more space, and a larger permissions budget, I'd have liked to have included 'Albion Market' from *Acrimony* and 'Litany' from *Approximately Nowhere* too.

'Albion Market' and 'From Kensal Rise to Heaven' are placed back to back in *Acrimony*, and form a kind of diptych: both are in unrhymed four-line stanzas; both use sustained and precise description to characterize mid-80s London, and both attempt to read into the cityscapes they present the spirit of the times underlying them. They share with, say, Martin Amis's fiction of this period the urge to diagnose a radical urban malaise, although it's a malaise for which it is clear that there is no cure: 'The surfaces are friable, broken and dirty, a skin unsuitable / for chemical treatment.' Hofmann's method in both these poems is to heap up instances of urban dysfunction that are then leavened with a wry, distinctive wit.

> Broken glass, corrugated tin and spraygunned plywood
>   saying
> *Arsenal rules the world.* Twenty floors up Chantry Point,
> the grey diamond panels over two arsoned windows
> were scorched like a couple of raised eyebrows.
>
> ('Albion Market')

The first three lines might be drawn from a TV documentary or newspaper report, but their impact is subtly modulated by that quirky final simile, with its almost defiant, dandyish flourish of the powers of the imagination. Indeed, there is a fascinated kind of relish in both poems' accumulation of images of sordidness and blight, for they seem to release in Hofmann a kind of compensatory humour, allowing him to demonstrate his ability to survive, and even flourish and begin to feel at home, in these unpropitious circumstances:

> A few streets away, in the renovated precinct,
> girls' names and numbers stood on every lamp-post,
> phone-booth, parking meter and tree. Felt tip on sticky
>   labels,
> 'rubber', and 'correction' for the incorrigible.
>
> ('Albion Market')

In 'Summer', collected in *Approximately Nowhere*, Hofmann describes himself as having or finding 'nowhere to grip in the slippery city'. Although the persona of these two earlier poems adopts a predominantly passive attitude to the carnival of prostitution and vandalism and economic failure to which they bear witness, a kind of jaunty brio keeps breaking through, as if the poems couldn't help but celebrate their own highly individual way of responding to the evidence offered on every street corner of violence and decay:

> Some Sunday mornings, blood trails down the street
> from the night before. Stabbing, punch-up or nosebleed,
> it's impossible to guess, but the drops fell thickly and
>   easily
> on the paving-stones, too many for the rules of hop-
>   scotch.
>
> ('From Kensal Rise to Heaven')

The joke, again, models a way of responding to, of getting a 'grip' on, the slippery city. Hofmann makes us vividly aware that he has taken the full measure of the slice of London life that surrounds him, but also of how his persona can find an imaginative purchase on the broken and dirty urban surfaces, rather like the 'rough-necked, microcephalous' pigeons that happily roost in an abandoned shop on Kensal Rise:

> The pigeons mate in full view: some preliminary billing,

> then the male flutters his wings as though to break a
>   fall . . .
> They inhabit a ruined chiropodist's, coming and going
>   freely
> through broken windows into their cosy excremental
>   hollow.

('From Kensal Rise to Heaven')

A weird kind of lyricism, then, seems to me to animate these poems, one that does full, even novelistic justice to the scenes described, yet also creates a space for the poet as a quizzical, uncertain, but imaginatively and politically engaged observer of this urban jungle. The conclusion of 'From Kensal Rise to Heaven' even gestures towards a version of the metropolitan sublime; all the streets' 'untidy activity', to use a phrase of Elizabeth Bishop's, is momentarily suspended, making way for a muted but effective yearning for the cosmic, conveyed through the angling of the various skylights towards the setting sun:

> The motor-mews has flat roofs of sandpaper or tarpaper.
> One is terraced, like three descending trays of gravel.
> Their skylights are angled towards the red East,
> some are truncated pyramids, others whole glazed shacks.

Both 'Albion Market' and 'From Kensal Rise to Heaven' create a poetic version of the 'glazed shack', from which the ruthless struggles for survival being acted out on the streets they describe can be observed, and then angled by the poet's off-beat humour. The urban persona Hofmann launches is acutely aware of what he calls in 'Malvern Road' 'the grim Tuesday *Guardian* Society-section aspect of it', but has not yet become inured to the menace and injustice that saturates urban life. An aspect of the poems' sophistication is their cherishing of their persona's naivety, and the access this naivety gives to vivid responses and impressions. How soon, both poems subliminally ask, before one gets so used to prostitutes' adverts and curb-crawlers and drunks, to blood on the streets and forbidding estates named after famous British writers ('Dickens House, Blake Court, Austen House'), that they no longer register sharply enough to furnish material for a poem? The freshness of 'Albion Road' and 'From Kensal Rise to Heaven' derives from the license to be impressed by the city at first-hand that is granted the newcomer, before residence has rendered one indifferent or blasé, and liable to respond to deprivation by making a quip about the Tuesday *Guardian*. And it is through his figuration of his naivety and curiosity that Hofmann attempts to make his persona endearing to the reader:

> *Joy, local*, it says in the phone-booth, with a number
> next to it. Or *Petra*. Or *Out of Order*, and an arrow.
> This last gives you pause, ten minutes, several weeks . . .
> Delay deters the opportunist as much as doubt.

It's another, perhaps slightly less appealing facet of this naivety that drives the rather adolescently tut-tutting tabloid-headline conclusion to 'Albion Market', with its denunciation of the entire country:

> . . . Game spirits, tat and service industries,
> an economy stripped to the skin trade. Sex and security,
> Arsenal boot boys, white slaves and the SAS.

'Well,' as a Philip Larkin line puts it, 'useful to get that learnt.'

The two London poems in *Approximately Nowhere*, though not printed back to back, also form a diptych, for both are written in unrhymed six-line stanzas, and in a single tumbling sentence that lasts in 'Malvern Road' for eight stanzas, and in 'Litany' for seven. If 'Albion Market' and 'From Kensal Rise to Heaven' communicate the excitement and wonder, shading at times into horror, of a newcomer to London, 'Malvern Road' and 'Litany' use the city to dramatize the excitement and wonder, shading at times into guilt, of an affair that propels the poet out of the 'cosy . . . hollow' of his life with his wife and his children, and back onto the streets. And if both emerge from what sometimes gets called a mid-life crisis, it's a crisis that involves a recovery of the energies of youth, as he makes clear when he compares himself to the May seeds of alder and plane and sycamore in 'Litany' – 'generative fluff, myself fluffy and generative, / wild-haired and with the taste of L. in my mouth'. 'Malvern Road' – which is in West Kilburn – is a flashback poem, a commemoration of, an elegy to, his early days in London with his wife Caroline, and is thus a recreation of the 80s London of the two *Acrimony* poems, a decade or so on, while in 'Litany' Hofmann finds himself plunged back into the bedsit land of the new arrival in London, following his departure from the family home. 'Dear god,' it opens:

> let me remember these months of transition
> in a room on the Harrow Road, the traffic
> muffled by a plastic sheet, the facing ziggurats
> with their satellite dishes and tea-towels out to dry,
> a lengthwise Brazilian flag curtaining one window,
>
> indigents and fellow aliens and oddballs in the street,
> the wobbly eyes I mistakenly looked into, wobbly and
> then
> suddenly murderous . . .

The break-up of his relationship has allowed Hofmann to recover that feeling of being an alien or oddball that underlay 'Albion Market' and 'From Kensal Rise to Heaven', and enabled him to convert his experiences of the city into poetry, just as it does here. The descriptive drive in Hofmann seems to depend fundamentally on a sense of displacement, to be inspired by his need to orientate and define himself in relation to whatever new territory he is exploring. The frontier here is of course emotional rather than geographical, for Malvern Road is only minutes away from the Harrow Road, as the opening of 'Malvern Road' points out – 'It's only a short walk, and we'll never make it'.

These *Approximately Nowhere* London poems share an almost hysterical forward propulsiveness that makes all they describe into a vehicle for the poet's own emotional high, meaning we experience the urban snapshots he offers as a kind of montage of images accompanying a sweeping crescendo of inner *sturm und drang*.

> the office workers opposite
> very evidently pissing behind milk-glass,
> goslings and baby coots without the white stripe as yet,
> attack dogs defecating on the grass,
> the occasional putter of narrowboats, industrial
> and bucolic as canals are industrial and bucolic,
>
> the velvet curtains slowly turning to dust on the wood-
>   wormed rail,
> my diminished establishment of bin-liners and suitcase
> (our 1961 cardboard family 'Revelation'),
> the Olympia Traveller I lugged around Mexico and two
>   pairs of boots,
> otherwise silence and light and dust and flies,
> so hungry I picked the bin when I visited my children . . .

This insistent, almost compulsive collaging of sights and sounds and memories resembles the closing sequence of a film, as it cuts from scene to scene, braiding all together into a composite self-portrait of the poet, leaving one life behind and on the verge of another, at an unsustainable pitch of excitement. London here becomes a city of romance, its heterogeneous mix of buildings and the strata of its history unreeling as brilliantly-lit backdrop to the personal drama the poet is staging for us, and its climax at nightfall, 'and the bus that took me round the houses / to heaven.'

'Malvern Road', on the other hand, is an elegiac recreation of an earlier romance, the one that led to the children mentioned in 'Litany'. It is the intensity of his recollection of things past that infuses the cityscapes it revisits with a desperate, poignant vividness. It's the 'Before' to 'Litany''s 'After', reframing the innocence and charged wonder with which the *Acrimony* poems respond to London like a first-time buyer, so to speak, but here with a rueful sense of time past, of life used up, of the impossibility of reliving the 'heartstopping fun' of being young in the city:

> probably we were happy but in any case
> we were beyond dreams in the strange actualness of
>   everything,
> a tyro salary, a baby mortgage, such heartstopping fun,
> the place too intimate and new and connected to us
> for us to think of 'entertaining'
> and we liked the stairs best of everything anyway . . .

The inverted commas around 'entertaining' might be taken as an illustration of the way the poem as a whole quotes from his youth as from an old diary, rather like Beckett's Krapp, reliving times past while overwhelmingly aware of the enormous gulf between now and then. The poem's double focus is mirrored in the fullness and fidelity with which it records the urban scene in which this hopeful marital odyssey was launched, while never quite letting us forget that these nostalgic vignettes are like so many photos in the family album of a couple who are now divorced:

how frightening everything was,
and with how much faith, effort and heart
we went out to meet it anyway,

the corner pub we probably never set foot in,
the health centre padlocked and grilled like an offie,
the prefab post office set down at an odd angle,
the bank that closed down, the undertaker who stayed
    open . . .

We learn of the rupture definitively only in the poem's final lines, which literally show a dream becoming a responsibility, a responsibility that the poet confesses, in a spasm of remorse, that he is now evading:

the pepper-fruited scrawny alder with two yellow days
    of pollen,
the nights of your recurring dream
where you whimpered comfort to your phantom baby
    boy
you didn't have and said you'd mind him, as now,
to my shame, you have and you do.

As always in Hofmann at his best, what is described – that 'pepper-fruited scrawny alder' – becomes a fitting and expressive extension of the persona incarnate in the poem, who, for all his seeming passivity and ineptness, gathers reality about him like a centripetal force. And focused by this persona, London emerges with a startling clarity and distinctiveness in these poems; taken together, and despite his protestations to the contrary, they exert a firm and compelling imaginative grip on the slippery city. They seem to me among the finest London poems of our era.

Pfauen am Broadway

1

Alles ist ein paar Nummern größer: Ein Himmel,
Der tief in die Straßen schneidet, Hydranten,
Mächtig wie Ochsenköpfe, die Landesfahne,
Im Seewind schwer wie ein Bettlaken flappend,
Ein Eistransporter, der vor der Kathedrale parkt.
Du schlägst die Augen auf und bist –
In Amerika. Neben dir sitzt ein Mexikaner,
Der im Bus ein Taschenbuch liest »In Gottes Hand«.
Alles ist ein paar Nummern größer, und Peter Pan
Summt dir ständig ins Ohr, kleiner Karl.

2

Und wie betritt man dies Land? O ich weiß, wie –
Durch die Tür der Kinderbücher zuerst,
Dann den Spalt in den Sternen, den Streifen.
Mit den spanischen Karavellen, mit Hundeschlitten
Über Alaskas eisige Flächen, den Yukon hinunter
Als Wolfsblut, entlang der Goldsucherlager
Von Saloon zu Friedhof. Indianerterritorium
War das Zauberwort für Kinder und Geographen.
Mit den Planwagen, den Auswandererschiffen,
Den ersten Eisenbahnen, die den Büffel vertrieben,
Zwischen Küste und Küste, mit einem Zeppelin,
Der leider in Flammen geriet und verbrannte.

Peacocks on Broadway

translation by ANDREW SHIELDS

1

Everything's a couple sizes bigger: a sky
Cutting deep into the streets, hydrants
As hefty as the heads of oxen, the country's flag
Flapping like a heavy sheet in the seawind,
An ice truck parked outside the cathedral.
You open up your eyes and you are in –
America. Beside you sits a Mexican
Reading a paperback on the bus: 'In God's Hand'.
Everything's a couple sizes bigger, and Peter Pan
Is always humming in your ear, little Karl.

2

And how can you enter this country? Oh, I know how –
First through the door of children's books,
Then the crack in the stars, the stripes.
With the Spanish caravels, with dog sleds
Across Alaska's icy plains, down the Yukon
As wolf blood, along the gold diggers' camps
From saloon to graveyard. Indian territory
Was the magic word for children and geographers.
With the covered wagon, the ships of emigrants,
The first railroads that scattered the buffalo,
Between coast and coast, with a Zeppelin
That sadly burst into flames and burned.

3

Dezemberkälte, und die Sonne brennt auf den Pelz
Der alten Damen im Central Park. Die eine trägt
Turnschuh zum Mantel, die andere Cowboystiefel.
Und alle sind sie geadelt in diesem Licht,
Das der Seewind reinigt, ein Magnum-Filter,
Der das Kleine für Groß erklärt, das Große zu etwas,
Das sich bald aus den Augen verliert, himmelwärts
Oder in Häuserfluchten. Wozu aufschauen,
Wo das Ungewöhnliche durch die Straßen zieht
Als eines von vielen Themen
Der Musik dieser Stadt. *Andante cantabile*,
Mit schleppenden Federn ging da, das Krönchen
Schief auf dem Kopf ein Pfau durch die Menge
Und noch ein Pfau und dann noch ein Pfau –
Drei truthahnfüßige, langsam schreitende Diven.
Woher nur, wohin? Die Leute von Harlem
Wußten es ebenso wenig wie die Leute von Queens.
Kein Zoo vermißte sie, auch nicht der geheime
Kräutergarten der neogotischen Kathedrale.
Dekadenz war hier billig zu haben, ein Angebot
Im Vorübergehen: Drei Stück zum Preis von einem.
Der Broadway nahm sie wie alles was sich bewegt.

4

Die Pferde am Südeingang Central Park,
Geschniegelte Fiakerpferde in einer Taxistadt,
Erkennen ihresgleichen in Bronze nicht wieder.
Sie ignorieren den Gaul, der sich aufgebäumt hat
Unter José Marti, Kubas heldischem Vollblut.

3

December cold, and the sun is burning on the furs
Of the old ladies in Central Park, one wearing
Sneakers with her coat, another cowboy boots.
And they are all ennobled in this light
The sea wind purifies, a Magnum filter making
Whatever's small much bigger and whatever's big
Into something quickly lost to sight, up to
The sky, or down the rows of houses. Why look up
When the unusual wanders the streets
As one of many themes
Of the music of this city. *Andante cantabile*,
Its feathers dragging, its little crown aslant
On its head, a peacock walked through the crowd,
And another peacock, and then another –
Three slowly striding, turkey-footed divas.
Where from? Where to? The people from Harlem
Knew that no more than the people from Queens.
No zoo had lost them, nor had the secret
Herb garden of the neo-Gothic cathedral.
Decadence could be had here cheap, an offer
Made in passing: three for the price of one.
Broadway took them, like everything that moves.

4

The horses at the south entrance to Central Park,
Dandified carriage-horses in a taxi city,
Don't recognize their kind in bronze.
They ignore the nag that's rearing up
Under José Marti, Cuba's heroic thoroughbred.

Sie tragen ihr Zaumzeug wie Showgirls das Mieder.
Sie begreifen nicht, was das Paraderoß soll,
Auf dem Simon Bolivar nach Downtown reitet.
Von dorther stürmt ihm Kosciuszko entgegen
Auf einem Rappen, glänzend wie nasser Asphalt.
Verkehr hielt ihn auf. Er hat sich verspätet
Beim Rapport mit George Washington
Unten im Union Square Park.

Reiter, wohin man sieht –
Roosevelt von der Kavallerie, General Slocum,
Jeanne d'Arc im Riverside Park, der Ritter El Cid.

Reiter im Regen, Reiter stürmen von allen Seiten
Die Plätze. Sie durchkämmen die Warenhäuser,
Sie sprengen durch Fußgängerströme,
Reiter auf Polizeipferden thronend,
Sie sprengen die Stadt.

Ein Schwarzer steht vor der Nationalbibliothek.
Ich will ein Reiterstandbild, schreit er.
Ein Mädchen mit Pferdeschwanz himmelt ihn an.
Ich auch, sagt sie leise, als Mama sie weiterzerrt.
Ein goldenes großes, so eins wie General
William Tecumseh Sherman.

5

Was für ein Wind ist das, der einen trägt
Und jeden hier Willkommen heißt?
Ein Wind, von Stimmen voll, Fragmenten
Aus einem Hymnus, den die Herkunft nährt
Und jede Straßenecke wie Papier zerreißt.

They wear the bridle like showgirls wear the bodice.
They don't get what the marching steed is up to
That Simon Bolivar is riding downtown.
With Kosciusko storming toward him,
On a black horse that shines like wet asphalt.
Traffic slowed him down. He was late
Reporting to George Washington
Down in Union Square Park.

Riders no matter where you look –
Roosevelt of the cavalry, General Slocum,
Jeanne d'Arc in Riverside Park, the knight El Cid.

Riders in the rain, riders storming the squares
From every direction. They rummage the department
    stores,
Blast through the streams of pedestrians,
Riders athrone on police horses,
Blasting away the city.

A black man outside the National Library.
I want a statue with a horse, he cries.
A ponytailed girl making eyes at him.
Me, too, she says softly, as Mama drags her on.
A large, golden one, one just like General
William Tecumseh Sherman.

5

What kind of wind is this that carries you along,
Making everyone welcome here?
A wind full of voices, fragments
Of a hymn the origin nourishes
And every street corner tears like paper.

Avenue of the Americas: das klang
Wie Zirkuswerbung aus den alten Tagen.
Ein Blick in Straßenschluchten, und eröffnet
War das Naturtheater für ein Flüchtlingskind,
Das gestern kam, sein Glück zu wagen.

All die Kassiererinnen in den Billigläden
Tanzten am Feierabend in den neuen Jeans.
Gefallne Engel klappten ihre Flügel nachts
Am Bahnsteig ein und fuhren in Quartiere,
Die fern in Brooklyn lagen und in Queens.

Spinner der Märchen, Phantasienweber,
Was sagt ihr zu den neusten Happy Ends?
Fragt man den Wind, der um die Ecken pfeift,
Spielt er den Hymnus wie aus alten Tagen,
Filtert aus Filmen die gelungenste Sequenz.

6

Polizeisirenen am Morgen, mittags das Gekreisch
Des entflogenen Ara im Village, bei Nacht
Ein Stöhnen aus Fahrstuhlschächten, das Ächzen
Der Mega-Tonnen verbrauchten Metalls, Dampf
Der aus Stahlplatten zischt im Asphalt: Erst im Schlaf
Wird das ganze in Orchesternoten gesetzt.

So vertraut ist der Sound dieser Stadt (woher rührt
Dies Vertrautsein) – wie der farbreiche Horizont
Einer Opernkulisse, die man fünf Akte lang sah.
Und war es nicht so, daß man in dicken Polstern
Den Broadway hinabglitt, konzertant umspielt
In der Loge, einer der sich in Schaufenstern sonnt?

Avenue of the Americas: that sounded
Like circus advertising from the old days.
A glance down the rows of buildings – and it opened,
The nature theater for a refugee child
Who arrived yesterday to test his luck.

All the cashiers in the discount stores
Danced at quitting time in their new jeans.
At night, the fallen angels folded their wings
On the platforms and rode out to neighborhoods
Far off in Brooklyn and in Queens.

Spinners of tales, fantasy weavers,
What do you say to the latest happy ends?
Ask the wind that whistles round the corners,
And it will play the hymn just like in the past
And pick the most successful sequence from the films.

6

Police sirens in the morning, at noon the shrieking
Of the fugitive macaw in the Village, at night
A moaning from elevator shafts, the groaning
Of megatons of used metal, steam
Hissing from steel plates in the asphalt: only in sleep
Is it all set in notes for orchestra.

So familiar, the sound of this city (where is this
Familiarity from) – like the colorful horizon
Of a set for an opera stared at for five acts.
And didn't you drift down Broadway
In thick cushions, the concert playing all around you
In the box, someone sunning in shop windows?

Endlich sah er, was der Name besagte, den Fleck
An den Küsten der Welt, der ins Maximum trieb.
Mannahatta, ein Indianerwort, das es in sich hatte,
Wie Himmelsbrot, von den höchsten Türmen verteilt.
Diamantenes Varieté des Regens auf dem Asphalt,
Den die Nacht blankwusch, bevor ein neuer Tag
Ihn mit den Komparsen aller Kontinente beschrieb.

Finally he saw what the name signified, the stain
On the coasts of the world that drove it to the max.
Mannahatta, an Indian word that had what it takes,
Like manna scattered from the highest towers.
The rain's diamond varieté on the asphalt
Is polished clean by the night before a new day
Writes on it with all the continents' extras.

The Exile of Not Exactly

RALPH JAMES SAVARESE

Michael had come to give a reading at the small Iowa college where I teach – it was as much an excuse to see me, his former student, as it was a chance to sell copies of his latest book. He was shocked, I think, by just how isolated the college is. Halfway between Des Moines, the capital, and Iowa City, where the University of Iowa is located, the town boasts a population of 9,000 and is surrounded on all sides by big, agribusiness farms. You can travel an hour in either direction on I-80, one of the highways that span the US, without seeing much of anything. You can travel downtown, for that matter, without seeing much of anything. And the food, well – let's not go there, as Americans like to say.

The Plains writer Gretel Erlich once titled a book *The Solace of Open Spaces*, but I have never found such openness a balm. The people seem small out here, small and bent to the core, like the scraggily pines they plant as a windbreak on their prairie homes' western borders. The fronts that come through, their endless histrionics, mock the tight-lipped stoicism of the locals. Stooping in spite of themselves, these locals seem to want to compensate for that great embarrassment of sky, that rotund relative who has forgotten what it means to be respectfully dour and repressed, which is to say Scandinavian. The weather in Iowa, I remember telling Michael, is like a Sharon Olds poem: entirely too confessional.

Michael knew I wasn't thrilled about being stranded on the Plains, but that's what the market did to newly minted PhDs: it flung them far and wide. Six years after completing an MFA, my doctorate in hand, I had set out for what mid-nineteenth-century America called the Iowa Territories – in little more than a prairie schooner, it seemed, wife and son in tow. I hadn't yet accommodated myself to my new surroundings. In fact, I was in the habit of being rather obnoxious about said surroundings. When the legislature held a competition for a new State motto, I repeated a colleague's mordant entries over and over: 'Iowa, the Turd World'; 'Iowa, Gateway to Nebraska'. (This second submission provoked a rebuke, with the tourism official deeming it 'gratuitously unkind.')

Michael found these little geographical jabs amusing, laughing in a way that reminded me of a look from class years before: 'Ralph, you're being inappropriate again, but I would be most pleased if you would continue in exactly this manner.' (OK, that's my rather self-serving translation.) When I told him that Iowa stands for 'Idiots Out Wandering Around' or, even better, 'I Oughta Went Around it', he laughed uproariously. Iowa has more hogs than people, for God's sake – methane gas is a monumental problem.

What Michael and I shared was a sense of exile. I would joke that Mao had sent me to a re-education camp in the countryside; he would joke that Thatcher had sent him to an X-rated Disneyworld. He, of course, spent half the year in Gainesville teaching at the University of Florida – what I still refer to as the University of Baywatch after that inane, beach-and-bikini-lifeguard-show on American television. When I was a teaching assistant at UF, I put a sign on my door that said, 'No shirt, no shoes, no *parka*, no service.' UF's ignoble savages, who would sometimes come to office hours in their bathing suits, left me dumbfounded. Where, may I ask, is an instructor to look when the young woman in front of him is practically nude?

The town seemed the oddest mix of porn and God. One Gainesville strip club called itself Café Risque; another, Tits 'n Grits – that's right, Tits 'n Grits. You had to buy breakfast to watch the ladies sans pajamas. Apparently they danced right above your huevos rancheros – on a bar that might otherwise have served alcohol. (I never went in, but it sure made me wonder: did the performers have to wear a different kind of hairnet?) Invariably, the same locale would sport an evangelical church, sometimes right next door. The threat of damnation lurked everywhere. Once, after I had embarrassed a former collegiate tennis player and current Baptist minister on the court, my forlorn opponent took a golden shovel out of his racket bag and invited me to bury my sins – I had behaved, he said, in a prideful manner. (The man would later be denounced on Palm Sunday by a parishioner with whom he was having an affair.)

At night the place could get scary; whatever hid during the day seemed to come out after dark – or, rather, to drop down from the sky like a giant palmetto bug. If you left anything unlocked, at least where I lived, it would be gone by morning. I never felt entirely comfortable walking around at night – something shady always seemed to be happening just a block in front of you.

Michael captures the sinister asininity of Gainesville in a poem entitled 'Freebird'. It begins like this:

> Six girls round the pool in Stranglers' weather,
> tanning; then three; then one (my favourite!),
> every so often misting herself
> or taking a drink of ice water from a plastic beaker.

Anyone familiar with the town knows of Danny Rolling, the serial killer who attacked UF students. My wife and I arrived in Gainesville just after the killings had stopped, though before the killer had been apprehended. We were sufficiently alarmed as to rent an apartment in the only high-rise condominium with a doorman. Later we would live across the street from a funeral home that contractually disposed of prisoners who had died or been executed and whose bodies had lain unclaimed

– 'Old Sparky', Florida's electric chair, was just up the road in a town called, appropriately enough, Starke. The serial killer Ted Bundy, for example, had been embalmed there. On more than one occasion, some friends and I were sitting on the front porch late at night when a delivery occurred – the State hearse strangely yellow, or so it seemed, a hornet on wheels.

In 'Freebird', the weary cosmopolitan, as a reviewer once referred to Michael, mischievously assumes the point of view of a Rolling-like figure, or perhaps I should say that the killer's psychological estrangement becomes a metaphor for the cosmopolitan's predicament – his percolating frustration, his palpable loneliness. Living abroad anywhere is alienating enough, but living abroad in Florida where, as Michael puts it in another poem, 'they give a man / five death sentences / to run more or less concurrently' and 'where little old ladies / squinny over their dashboards / and bimble into the millennium, with cryogenics to follow', well, that's just too surreal to make sense of.

The setting of 'Freebird' is

> a blue by pink downtown development,
> Southern hurricane architecture in matchwood:
> live-oaks and love-seats, handymen and squirrels,
> an electric grille and a siege mentality.

Leave it to Michael to use the word 'love-seat' in this context; 'handyman', too. Rolling, after all, had been a 'handyman', someone all too handy at entering through a locked, sliding glass door.

I've been to that shoddy 'blue by pink development' – Michael rented a place there year after year despite its being overrun by drunken ignorami. A little pig's house of straw, it could have been blown down by any category 2 wolf. In the poem, the culture's 'siege mentality' finds its ironic reflection in a speaker who says of himself and of his early days in Gainesville:

> I was cuntstruck and fat. My tight chinos
> came from a Second Avenue surplus store
> that had an RPG dangling from the ceiling.

The poem cleverly evokes threats from within and without –
part phallic antagonist, part human war trophy, the RPG almost
seems to flirt with the speaker.

I never understood why, beyond mere convenience, Michael
chose to live where he lived. If readers of his exquisitely refined
translations knew the setting in which he produced many of
them, they would shake their heads and laugh. 'Freebird' concludes with the memory of a 'fratboy overhead g[iving] it to
his sorority girl steamhammer style'. As Lynyrd Skynyrd blasts
away in the background, the girl's 'little screams peter[] out,
inachevée'. By conflating audible pleasure with inaudible death,
the poem affirms its ghoulish joke: the speaker would like to kill
these people. Irony, it turns out, is the ultimate cosmopolitan: it
manages to do what the speaker cannot: reconcile incommen-
surate perspectives, feel at home in both.

Of course, Michael never really took up residence in that
apartment – or in any of the others that followed. 'I lived in
three bare rooms and a walk-in refrigerator,' he declares wryly.

> The telephone kept ringing for Furniture World.
> I looked at the dirty waves
> breaking on the blue carpet and said not exactly.

When I think of Michael, I think of him as forever without
furniture, undecorated, certainly unconditioned. (The air in
Florida, the inside air, seems to have been shipped in straight
from corporate Antarctica.) Only recently, after buying a house
in Gainesville, has he succumbed to the custom of populating a
space with human-serving objects.

The exile of 'not exactly' – this is Michael's proper home. It's as much a constitutional stance as a political conviction, whether the politics be actual or literary. Recall his principled thrashing of a book by Donald Justice, for which he took flak from colleagues at UF where Justice had taught, or of the more recent translation of the collected poems of Zbigniew Herbert. If Michael doesn't admire something, he won't mince words, and it matters not a wit if you're friend or foe.

The opposite is true, too, however: when he does admire something, he becomes its indefatigable champion. For instance, he never really cared for my poems, but after I sent him the first chapter of my prose book *Reasonable People*, he spotted an editor on a London street corner, ran after her, and insisted that she read it immediately. The next day, the woman called from a ferry to Brittany and offered me a contract. Of course, my guardian agent refused to take credit for this or even to be thanked.

With adjustment, 'not exactly' is also how we might conceive of Michael's philosophy of translation. During a roundtable on his first trip to Iowa, he suggested that a translation ought to manifest a literary work's difficult passage into another language and culture. I took him to mean that the reader ought to be able to sense the transcontinental flight and three-hour wait at customs. He ought to be able to sense the language-lag, which is to say that a journey has been undertaken and a new world discovered. The word 'translation', after all, finds its origin in the phrase 'to bear across', as in to convey a saint to heaven. I don't believe that Michael has made this point in print, though I'm enormously attracted to it (especially if we conceive of a smooth yet impossibly long linguistic flight).

He has, however, explicitly resisted 'functional' understandings of translation, where the translator is anything but an agent in his own right. To most people, translation, he laments, is 'not fully personalized and accredited work. No one sees it. You're an ambulance driver, not a surgeon.' He 'want[s] it to matter that a book has had [his] time and [his] English expended on it, and not someone else's'. He 'want[s] both the choice of book, and the manner of the translation, to be expressive of [him]'. Thus, he has no patience at all for those pushing literal fidelity. Responding to a reader who took him to task for a translation of Gottfried Benn, Michael avers:

> There is no more dismal – or, frankly, stupid – way of reading a translation than to pick on single words (as though the first duty of a translation were that it should be reversible – it's not – and as though words were tokens of unchanging value, the way money used to be, in its dreams – they're not either) . . . I don't see how I could have served Benn any better in English, both in large and in little. My 'choices' (detestable word) are absolutely 'the best available' (certainly to me), and if they can be improved, then at least it won't be by any obvious so-called 'literal' so-called 'dictionary equivalents.'

'Not one of the things I have done is a liberty, or even close,' Michael concludes. 'I have merely said things the way they get said in English, precisely, and with tact.'

Precisely, not exactly. This difference makes, as it were, all the difference: two traditions in the world of letters communicate through the intervention of a translator – through, as Michael puts it elsewhere, the 'strange bi-authorship of translation'. As he pointed out in an OpEd bemoaning the end of the foreign language requirement in English secondary education, now more than ever, the globe needs such cooperation: 'Surely, apart from anything else, with more language-learning, there would have been fewer wars over the past decades?' Preposterous as it might be to try, imagine Blair and Bush studying Arabic, even translating Iraqi poetry. Imagine pens and word processors, not tanks and fighter jets, as the communicative instruments of choice.

In a poem entitled 'Letter from Australia', published in the

London Review of Books and dedicated to his former wise-guy student, Michael fancies, if only for a few moments, an exile so geographically removed from the center of Anglo-American imperialism that his anger and frustration at the state of things might abate. It was the run-up to the 2008 election – McCain vs. Obama. Michael had been out to Iowa a second time, joined by our dear friend Peter Sokol. The District Court of Iowa had ruled that marriage licenses cannot be denied on the basis of sexual orientation – to the delight of nearly everyone at my college and to the dismay of the State's many right-wing evangelicals. (The Supreme Court would unanimously uphold this ruling, paving the way for gay marriage, though successful recall elections for a number of justices would follow.) The price of gas was alarmingly high, and farmers were downright giddy about the prospects for that corn-based alternative, ethanol.

The poem begins aubade-like, but something is askew:

> The early worm gets the bird –
> it's morning in Australia.
> It's strange to be so bilious
> so far away.
>
> Little to do with Australia,
> which as far as I can see
> seems mostly delightful:
> airy pastel buildings and trees I can't name.

After pondering a number of local problems, which seem utterly trivial, even quaint, when compared to the corruption and dishonesty some seven thousand miles away, the speaker at last identifies the source of his biliousness:

> And still we wake haunted by
> the familiar American *galère*:

Cheney the sinisterly skewed orangutan,
the worn charmlessness of Bush,
the clumping one-armed snowman McCain,
looking either to club or hug.

And now – the commentariat agog
at the promised melange of snowsports and watersports –
Sarah P., the driller killer
the uterine shooterine.

The poet's parodic rhymes, his verve, nearly neutralize the truc-
ulent absurdity of conservative politics. 'If you can have Little
Englanders,' the speaker asks,

can't you have Little Americans,
half-awash with Washington's hormones,
half in rebellion against them?

And so the private anthem morphs from 'not exactly' to 'not at
all'.

   The poem then concludes with an apostrophe, and we come
full circle – with Michael remembering the joke I had once told
him about the acronym that is IOWA:

My friend in the bonsai liberal exclave
in your biodiesel flyover state,
I can still register my first
Zolaesque frisson of horror

at the fried turnip smell of the cars
that ate not Paris, but whatever you called it –
I Oughta Went Around It.
There is no going around it.

This recognition paradoxically fuels Michael's restive itinerancy – his movement a counter to that of global American hegemony, not a reflection of, or escape from, it. Michael, it probably need not be said, has never gone around anything, and in friendship he has never, not once, been an expat.

At the end of his second trip to Iowa, I drove him to the airport in Des Moines. The unusually warm, sunny weather had turned: it was snowing furiously. I-80 took on that *Dr Zhivago* quality, only updated with tanker trucks and the careless skirmishing of red and white compact cars. Michael was about to commence an essay on Joseph Brodsky – yet another exile, Brodsky, of course, was one of his heroes. Two days later, I received an email from Michael asking if he had left a book by Brodsky at my house – he hadn't. 'The book must be in the airport,' he wrote, and I remember thinking how plaintively ironic that was. Brodsky – or, rather, his poems waiting for their flight.

The Transport of Bunker Oil

SARAH MAGUIRE

The big tanker eases up the Bosphorus in the small hours,
dark limb shrugging off dark water, implacable,
little silken pleats of silver in its wake. Silent.
Like a mythical creature dreaming its passage
to the afterlife. Thrice an hour they head north,
crowned by a scant rig of lights, a busted
constellation; the bridge a brick of yellow light,
manned, the heart of it all, while the able seamen
sleep below decks, bunks snug against piping,
the continuous roar of the engines like the rush
of a mother's blood coursing past the placenta,
white noise of the unborn child. The particulates
of bunker oil – heavier than gasoline or naphtha,
blackened by asphaltenes, so viscid that chill
turns it solid – stream into the air of Istanbul,
donating their particular tang: carcinogens.
It is interminable this traffic of cargo taken from
The Dardanelles through the throat of Constantinople
to the open-mouthed Black Sea ports. Climb to the top
of the Byzantine walls at Yedikule and a flotilla
of tankers at anchor seeds the Sea of Marmara,
squat pieces of oil on the tides' board in formation,
waiting to be played, to be ushered to Asia.
From the top of the last hill in Europe, I watch
this river of oil trawl northwards. That dog again,
and the adjacent rooftop nightclub with its spool
of dinner jazz – counterpoint to the carbon-rich thrum
of a city in reprieve before dawn. At my feet, a bridge,
where once a chain was cast across The Golden Horn.

Michael Hofmann's Disappearing Acts

DAVID WHEATLEY

According to Theodor Adorno, punctuation marks are 'traffic signals'. If 'exclamation points are red, colons green' and 'dashes call a halt', the role of the ellipsis is less immediately obvious. 'Diverted traffic', perhaps, down a convenient side-street of reverie and aposiopesis. Adorno's verdict is stern: surging in popularity during the Impressionist age, the ellipsis became the mark of commercialized free association, the typographical designation of a mood the writer had failed to conjure in words alone. Stefan George and his followers, he notes, were fond of shortening the conventional three dots to two but Adorno is unconvinced, inexactitude, he feels, being the (literal) point of the ellipsis. All of which suggests the Frankfurt School Marxist might have had harsh things to say of Michael Hofmann's poetry, whose relationship to the ellipsis has been one of unabashed addiction.

The first sentence of the first poem in Hofmann's first book ends with an ellipsis (the first of 84 over 48 pages, by my count): 'Having your photograph on my bedside table / is like having a propeller there . . .' From its bedside photograph 'Looking at You (Caroline)' moves on to more harrowing fare, with photographs of the Russian revolution and 'Eisenstein-faced peasants with red pupils . . .', their story trailing away into war, starvation and who knows what. Returning to Caroline *disparue*, our speaker senses the propeller may be turning already, imagining her 'stasis as whir, movement in perfect phase, / just before it starts walking backwards . . .' 'I am walking backwards into the future like a Greek', wrote Michael Longley, remembering the Greeks' sense of the future as lying behind them, and it is a bleakly modern landscape of dual carriageway and *Autobahnen* into which Caroline would seem to have vanished, with only the names on the signposts as clues as to her whereabouts: 'Nürnberg 100; Würzburg / (home of the Volkswagen) 200; Berlin 500 . . .' The name becomes a stand-in for the thing itself, as the pioneers of aviation learned, described in the poem's closing lines as 'never alone – / they named their machines after their loved ones.'

Should we take comfort in the signifier edging the signified out? We should not. The speaker of a Michael Hofmann poem is invariably aware of something having gone missing, leaving, if not a signpost, then the Hansel-and-Gretel breadcrumb trail of the ellipsis to point us in its general direction. A quick litany of the lost turns up the 'regrets . . .' of a late-night TV watcher ('Dependants'), the 'souvenir of your lovely blush . . .' ('Touring Company'), Japanese love-making behind a leather curtain 'flapping like a ventilator . . .' ('Museum Piece'), the lost wedded bliss somewhere beyond 'your meat-and-two-veg sex, / the occasional *Sauerbraten* . . .' ('*Hausfrauenchor*'), to go no further than *Nights in the Iron Hotel*. The first example in *Acrimony* occurs in 'Ancient Evenings' and conjures, as do so many of these examples, the question of lost or vanishing time: 'Not for long, not for a long time now . . .'

Time is not all that vanishes, and punctuation too is far from eternal. A strong subtext of Adorno's 'Punctuation Marks' is that, not just their written forms, but our feelings themselves have cultural histories, to which punctuation in its wordless way bears witness. Nicholson Baker has elegized lost Victorian punctuation marks, em dashes with colons and semi-colons attached like a dog's dangling bits, now relegated to the lumber room of history alongside the moustache cup and the fob-watch. Punctuation marks do more than answer existing emotional nuances, they simultaneously shape and condition them: if Ian McEwan characters are unable to linger over the languorous '—:'s and '—;'s beloved of Trollope, this may be a civilizational shift and not for the better either (the zombie laugh of the emoticon not-withstanding). How different is the exclamation mark in Span-ish, for instance, a language required to signal its excitement at the beginning as well as the end of a sentence, as Hofmann will have learned if he kept the promise in 'Guanajato Two Times' to learn the Spanish for 'Hullo, it's me again!' Where his ellipses are concerned, Hofmann will sometimes lack the patience to wait for a sentence to end: '*Gruppenbild ohne Dame*' and 'Family Holidays', on facing pages of *Nights in the Iron Hotel*, employ the elliptic fade-up, poetic eye-contact made across the bar before the chat-up line ('. . . A male Trinity, the Father and his two Sons', '. . . Every day I swam further out of my depth'). An oc-cupational risk for connoisseurs of the dash is exceeding two per sentence, at which point the hierarchy of main versus sub-clause becomes visually compromised, but with his affixed el-lipses Hofmann too will frequently dissolve the discrete unit of the sentence into the larger temporal flux of *temps perdu*. I dream of a Hofmann poem where the ellipses win their war on the surrounding words, expelling them altogether and leaving us with a page of nothing but punctuation marks, like the page of commas and full-stops Apollinaire appended to a book, to twit readers who had complained of their absence.

Another comparison for the ellipsis might be the line of bub-bles emitted by an underwater swimmer. Having jumped off the end of one clause, the Hofmann poem can surface in unexpect-ed places. 'Kif' jumps from an optician's shop to 'Heimito von Doderer's excursus on tobacco', and 'Shapes of Things' from the 'small outboard swastika' of a whale's 'whirling genitals' to Ava Gardner in *On the Beach*. More usually in *Acrimony* though, we sense the ellipsis marking an awkward moment in conversation, fingers drummed on a table-top or drags on a cigarette. In the political poems of that volume's first half, fretting in Thatcher's shadow, it reads as a wan attempt to join up its own dots in a fractured and winded world. More often though, like *The*

Waste Land on Margate Sands, the ellipsis can connect nothing with nothing. In 'Campaign Fever', the 'millionaire [Dennis Thatcher]'s statutory one idea' of cleaning railway tracks with sheep-dip nudges the poem towards politics before peace is restored in a wilting *faux*-pastoral vision: 'When he sold his shares, they grew neglected, / plants break out and reclaim the very pavements . . .' When the departed rail passenger finds herself, in the final lines, 'up to your eyes in a vigorous, / delinquent haze of buttercups, milfoil and maple scrub', this is not nature *redivivus*, this is entropy entering its vampire stage. The poem reaches a conclusion (a terminus, even) in which nothing is concluded, reinforcing our suspicion that it is in their midstream fugues and errancies that Hofmann's poems are in fact most fully present.

Winnie in *Happy Days* is an 'interrupted being', according to Beckett, who pebble-dashes the text of that play with ellipses *passim*. With the younger Hofmann who stalks the second part of *Acrimony*, the being is *in* the interruptions, one is tempted to feel, karate-chop line-breaks and all: 'I acquiesced in all our deaths . . .', 'so many things // were undependable . . .', 'Family was abasement // and obligation . . .', 'I proudly bought a copy on my expenses, giving you / your first royalties on twenty-odd years of my life . . .', 'My father peers into the lit sitting-room / and says, "Are you here?" . . .' When the poet answers this last question in the affirmative the father stalks back out again without a word, as though the prospect of actual conversation has contravened some unspoken rule of the Hofmann universe. There is a Beckettian moment of sorts later on, echoing that other interrupted character, Krapp, when 'Author, Author' describes Hofmann senior's characters as 'talkers in soliloquies, notebooks, tape-recordings, last wills . . .' We feel an accelerating sense of time running out, and when 'Author, Author' snorts out one last vignette of Gert Hofmann, 'A performance, like everything else . . . What's the point?', Hofmann could just as easily be talking about himself and the complicity of his endless 'points' in the patriarch's autumnal psychodrama. If so, it is no accident that he changes tack for the poem's conclusion, shifting from ellipses to three jabbing questions instead. Two poems on, the collection's final poem, 'Old Firm', also ends on three unanswered questions.

The shift appears to have been decisive. Ellipses are thinner on the ground in *Corona, Corona* and *Approximately Nowhere* (scarcely a dozen in the latter), and Hofmann begins to dally instead with stepped-line tercets and intralineal spacing. So many ways to twitch, fidget and fail to stay in one place! Then by the time of the section of 'New Work' in *Selected Poems* the ellipsis has disappeared altogether. 'The sighs of the Pléiade, planets in love, / mouthsounds, genie, come . . .', runs the final example in *Approximately Nowhere*, commandeering Rimbaud's 'Génie' to signal its itch to be gone. That was in 1999, since when his disappearing act has gone a lot further than a signature typographical slither. An ill-at-ease presence on the 1994 New Generation team sheet, before long Hofmann decided he wasn't playing ball after all. *Selected Poems* appeared eight years after *Approximately Nowhere*, and at the time of writing there is still no new collection in sight. Has there been a more spectacular piece of performative abstentionism in recent times? I say 'performative', as this period of silence has been punctuated not just by Hofmann's lava-like flow of translations, but also by prose dispatches from the land of the unpoem such as his 2004 *Poetry* manifesto, or anti-manifesto, 'Sing Softer: A Notebook'. T. S. Eliot insisted that the English language should be approached 'with antagonism' by anyone hoping to write well, but Hofmann's antagonism seems to reach the anger-management-issues level when he improves on Marianne Moore's 'I, too, dislike it' with 'I sometimes wonder if there are any poets who "like" it, and whether I would like them [. . .] It would seem to me to be like "liking" the new York Stock Exchange or the FTSE.'

His naturally elliptic character aside, Hofmann's CV already marks him out as a test case for the contemporary canon and its strong residual attachment to nationally demarcated traditions. How 'in' but not 'of' a tradition can a writer be, even in our age of comfy stretch-pants-like inclusiveness? The phrase 'Michael Hamburger, better known as a translator . . .' sums up fairly acutely the decades-long attempt of a previous German-born poet to insinuate himself in Anglo-Saxon bosoms. For his part, Hofmann has admitted that England lies somewhere at the 'edge of my circle', while in 'Sing Softer' he talks of his reluctance, as a reader, to take new writers on, the most recent Anglophone admission to his private canon being that fresh-faced debutant, James Schuyler. Once again, the compass reads 'approximately nowhere', betwixt and between languages, countries, traditions. Just about the last thing anyone could accuse Hofmann of being is twee, but in one of the new pieces from *Selected Poems*, 'Broken Nights', we find him cosying up to the Anglo-Saxon tradition with mock-twee knowingness: 'Groping for a piss, / As the poet saith', the poet being the Larkin of 'Sad Steps'. For a non-native speaker questions of tone are always tricky to negotiate, but here as elsewhere there is something principled and delicious in Hofmann's insistence on the slightly off-key, ill-at-ease flavour of his English (since when was anyone's radio the 'wireless' he waits to turn on?). Words fall apart in his hands ('Seducer mellotrons / What's a tron, mellow I can do?'), German obtrudes combatively ('Or merely / Dependency inducing / And *wehrzersetzend*'), and the poem ends on a note of near-nonsense ('Arise / Decline, Sir / Baa Bedwards'). In these recent poems, the now Florida-based Hofmann resembles nothing so much as a long-haul traveller still on trans-Atlantic time sitting down for a late-night beer at dawn, European time, and hatching some new dialect from the Babelian polyphony that is his life (the last poem in *Selected Poems* provides Hofmann with the sustenance for just such a scene, 'Styrofoam beaker of coffee, / refill, refill, and a spot of red-eye gravy'). Hofmann's habit of letting his poems trickle away down the plug hole of ellipses may be behind him, but these days he needs no typographical props to facilitate his vanishing acts. He is contemporary poetry's most flitting and elusive ghost, the white whale of our lost alternative to all that is provincial and small in a tawdry world, our impossible strong enchanter, the man who isn't there.

The Translator

ROBIN ROBERTSON

He will go west
and west again,
striking out on his own
in open water.
Sewing the surface,
one quarter man
three quarters verb,
fitting his turbulence
to the undertow.

'The Whole Fountaining Pack'

MEG TYLER

In his review of Robert Lowell's *Collected Poems* (*London Review of Books*, September 2003), Michael Hofmann writes of his epiphanic experience in first reading Lowell:

> To vary what Mallarmé says about himself (Lowell quotes it in his last book, *Day by Day*), here was someone who had the good fortune to find a style that made writing possible.

In writing of Lowell's style, Michael's own inimitable one reveals itself. I cannot locate a piece of his writing that does not find its style, from his reviews of the American poets he loves or hates to his discussion of the fiction writers he translates. Metaphors enliven the paragraphs:

> Making a choice is itself invidious in what is called a *Collected Poems*, though in Lowell's case probably unavoidable. Most poets hold out a card; Lowell seems to offer the whole fountaining pack.

The card metaphor is particularly apt for Lowell when we think back to his imitation of Sappho's 'Phanetai Moi':

> I set that man above the gods and heroes –
> all day, he sits before you face to face,
> like a cardplayer. Your elbow brushes his elbow –
> if you should speak, he hears.

Metaphor aside, what his writing reveals to us is that Michael is very good at hearing, at listening for the idiom, both in English and when trying to find an English equivalent for a German phrase. Idiom is the 'specific character or individuality of a language; the manner of expression considered natural to or distinctive of a language; a language's distinctive phraseology' (*OED*). When reading Michael's (among other) translations in *Twentieth-Century German Poetry: An Anthology* (2005), it may come as a surprise to some that the sensibilities that inhabit this book are recognizable. We also hear phrases that feel companionable to the ear, that create an intimacy of voice rather than a distance:

> . . . Funerals in summer. No let-up now.
> You meet acquaintances, and after ten years
> of not seeing each other, you always start off
> on the wrong foot, with mistaken identities;
> at least you're still able to make the exit
> under your own steam.
>
> ('. . . Funerals in summer', Jürgen Becker)

Perhaps his coming at English from his particular vantage point makes him more sensitive to turns of phrase than a monolingual speaker would be. He is alert to the different way the idioms can be heard. In this poem, the funerals come as frequently ('no let-up'), one supposes, as summer rain. He uses enjambment to illustrate the wrong-footedness of the encounter: 'start off /on the wrong foot' (and speaking of feet, the meter at the beginning of the fourth line is like one of Lowell's 'iambs loosened into anapests'). Another idiom appears in the sixth line ('under your own steam') and the presence of these contrasts with the absence of them in the German original (followed by my literal translation):

. . . Beerdigungen im Sommer. Jetzt hört es
nicht mehr auf. Man trifft Bekannte, und
das Wiedererkennen, nach wenigstens zehn Jahren,
beginnt mit Verwechslungen; immerhin, man kennt sich
noch aus zwischen Eingang und Ausgang.

[. . . Funerals in summer. It doesn't stop
anymore. Meeting people you know and
recognize after at least ten years,
starting with mistaken identities, but still
knowing the entries and exits.]

Michael's distinctive use of idioms helps to set the resigned but
comical tone of the passage. The knowledgeable levity is something we overhear not infrequently in his own writing. Michael
has a keen awareness of the comedy in English phrasing but
none of the non-native speaker's occasional blankness of comprehension or mistaken identity. We feel confident he knows the
entries and exits.

From his introduction to the recently published *Joseph Roth:
A Life in Letters*, Michael writes: 'We read for knowledge and
atmospheres, but also for the chance to develop and exercise empathy, to extend the weft and warp of our emotions and nerves
over the situations of others.' Is this not true of the whys and
wherefores of translation? For me, his *Twentieth-Century German Poetry* has had a kind of once-in-a-lifetime transformative
effect. I found a body of German lyric poets whose sensibilities
spoke to my own, in their separate sadnesses, their spare and wry
comments.

But back to idiom, and idiom used consciously. To take one of
many examples, from a poem he has translated by Durs Grünbein ('Titian's New Pad'), the last phrase reads, 'Frag die Fische,
sie schweigen' [Ask the fish, they are quiet.]. Michael's version
reads 'Don't take my word for it then, ask the fishes.' (The 'then'

extends the huff of this indignant response). He brings into the poem an engaged conversational tone that teases at the boundaries between prose and poetry.

His own prose excites and meanders, the sentences always heading in unexpected and edifying directions; the surprises remind me of the rare occasion when poets do something new and invigorating with rhyme. Hofmann achieves a similar effect with his compounding of phrases; the pairings, sometimes improbable, always apt, find their truths in unlikely juxtapositions. You cannot guess where he is going to go next. Maybe this comes from reading a lot of Lowell and a lot of Benn. In the Preface to *Joseph Roth: A Life in Letters*, he writes'

> Roth is both contradictory and changeable, and always, always vehement with it.
>
> Something in him can't abide and doesn't understand hierarchies; [. . .] He drinks to dull his nerves, and writes to understand the world. He is industrious from despair, assiduous and ineffectual, a tireless, incorruptible, terrifying and quixotic moralist.

In these few lines (alliterative, one can add: **d**rinks to **d**ull, in**d**ustrious from **d**espair, assi**d**uous) Hofmann offers a compact biography of Roth. The contrariness of Roth's nature appears in the pairing of contrary phrases: industry born out of despair, being at once 'assiduous' and 'ineffectual'.

The more I read Michael's translations, the more I tangle him up with the original authors. Am I reading Benn or am I reading Hofmann? But maybe this is not a bad thing. Stephen Mitchell's Rilke to me *is* Rilke; perhaps because it was the first edition of the poems I read, I find them to sound 'most like Rilke'. One of the definitions of translation offered by the *OED* is 'removal from earth to heaven, *orig.* without death'. This is what a good translation does for those of us who do not read the language in question – takes a text that is recognizable, for example, as a poem, but not comprehensible and makes it a transcendent and compelling work of art. If, as Rosanna Warren puts it, 'All real poetry is . . . writing in the light of death' then in translation the death of one sense gives life or light to another. Or in Michael's case, sundry lights.

Even when I do not have the German original in front of me, the English version impresses me as a poem in its own right. Here is Benn's 'Last Spring' ('Letzter Frühling'):

> Fill yourself up with the forsythias
> and when the lilacs flower, stir them in too
> with your blood and happiness and wretchedness,
> the dark ground that seems to come with you.
>
> Sluggish days. All obstacles overcome.
> And if you say: ending or beginning, who knows,
> then maybe – just maybe – the hours will carry you
> into June, when the roses blow.

> (*Poetry*, March 2011)

We can place the poem in the long tradition of those, like wretched Catullus ('Miser Catulle'), that offer the self advice (which must perforce occur in a moment of crisis, the poem a call for the return of a former and usually much-missed state of mind). 'Last' can refer to this past spring but it also hints at the last spring the speaker might ever experience. The mixing of 'blood and happiness and wretchedness' reminds me that Benn, like Hofmann, groups opposites. His sensibility does not shy away from the horrible or the beautiful, or a composite of the two. (This is a compound you find throughout Hofmann's writing, which does not seek uplift as much as insight.) The days slow down, become 'sluggish'; all that needs doing has been done, as seen in the nicely assonant 'obstacles overcome'.

Without tension, energy saps. Does spring signify an end or a beginning? It doesn't much matter, says Benn in the English translation. Michael's version of another Benn poem, 'Circulation' (*Paris Review*, Winter 2011), reads:

> The solitary molar of a streetwalker
> whose body had gone unclaimed
> had a gold filling.
> All the rest were gone,
> as if by tacit agreement.
> This one the morgue attendant claimed for himself,
> flogged it, and had himself a night out on the proceeds.
> Because, so he said,
> Only dust should revert to dust.

The title – and knowing Benn was a doctor – makes us think of blood moving round (although no longer in the streetwalker, alas), and also of how what goes round comes round. Even though I do not have the original, I am almost certain that 'had himself a night out on the proceeds' is Michael's idiosyncratic choice of idiom. I like the quiet soundplay and paralleling: 'solitary' and 'streetwalker' in the first line, 'dust' and 'dust' in the last. Even 'flogged it' seems like the phrase *juste* – selling, beating, being beaten – these are all things that chime with the streetwalker's trade.

Sometimes he appears to sacrifice some of the sound correspondence of the original for the sake of an idiomatic phrase that works on different levels. From *Twentieth-Century German Poetry*, one four-line poem by Inge Müller reads:

> Ich habe dich heute Nacht verlassen
> Für lange Zeit, mir ist: für immer.
> Der Morgen war ein graues Zimmer
> Und als du gingst war Rauch in den Strassen.

I left you last night
For a long time – I have a feeling, for good.
The morning was a grey room
And when you went out the streets were full of smoke.

'For good', meaning *for always* as well as *for what is best*. The *abba* rhyme scheme recalls the *rima baciata* of Petrarch, fitting for a poem about lost love, or love abandoned. In the original you have sound linkage between 'Zeit' and 'Zimmer' (time and room), as well as in the matching pair of prepositions in line two ('für'), which Michael replicates, adding a third fricative in 'feeling'. 'Good' and 'room' are off rhymes but he chooses not to work for a sound linkage at the end of lines 1 and 4. In choosing to end with 'smoke' instead of 'streets', he decides to bypass a possible off rhyme with 'night'. Somehow the open vowel sound in 'smoke' allows the poem an exit which suggests at the same time an opening out.

As to the question of sound, Richard Sieburth writes in *The Art of Translation: Voices from the Field* (edited by Rosanna Warren): 'As I now look back on my translations of Hölderlin, it is above all the space *between* my English and his German that occupies me [. . .] I can occasionally see the faint traces of my own words reaching through the palimpsest.' As a translator, he discovered he could but 'offer temporary hospitality to Hölderlin's errant original, to have it over as a guest for a while, to experience the communion of simple adjacency, one language sharing a moment of silence with another'. While I believe Michael appreciates silence, his silences do not always imply respect but reticent judgment, the raised eyebrow. In the spaces between the originals and Michael's translations, I discern a lively chattering coming from somewhere on the right.

It seems unfair to pore over translations the same way that one provides exegeses of original poems. Not to say that the poet's work isn't tricky, but the translator has more to prove, and perhaps more to lose. It is not his or her poem to begin with, but by the end it has more or less become so, and it will be judged by other translations or native speakers who hanker for literal versions. What is significant about Michael's achievement is that he has brought into English a century's worth of poetry – of European sensibility – that readers of English may otherwise have never encountered and hence have never understood how much we are alike.

Not that this recognition of our similitude was Michael's goal. He keeps an eye on outsiders. Of Elizabeth Bishop, Hofmann writes:

> She wasn't a player – she wasn't even American, but three parts Canadian. She had spells in New York and Washington, but she didn't (as she might have said) 'get on' in those places, and preferred the less assertive, more unregarded comers of Maine and Key West, where the US seems, a little improbably, to fade, and concede some of its identity to its neighbours . . .
>
> (*London Review of Books*, September 2011)

This living on the borders of places, where one country 'fades' into the next, is perhaps one aim of good translation, to make the other seem familiar. The translator wants the other way of seeing or imagining to enter our sensibility. It requires artfulness to be convincing. Like Bishop, who also translated poems (though only a limited number), Hofmann has lived in many landscapes – European and American – and listened to many languages, which makes him a man of various view. He is also a poet who likes writers as different as Lowell and Schuyler, Brecht and Fallada, although the voices differ substantially. On occasion I catch a quick glimpse of Hofmann as he hightails it round a corner, but for the most part I am utterly convinced by the authority of Roth's wry voice, the potboiler (and unbearable) quickness of Fallada.

I sometimes wonder what it must be like to live so deeply in two languages, to be inhabited by the intensity of these voices. The thought terrifies me in a way. To have that many voices housed in one head must be both inspiring and at times overwhelming. I am grateful he has taken on the task. Through Michael, I have grown to love German more than I did before. When I read it to myself, I hear Michael's voice reading. More impressively perhaps, reading Michael's nimble translations has made me see anew the astonishing dexterity of English sentences and lines.

What Michael has, beyond skill, is a quality of generosity, this carrying across of another human sensibility onto the page. This is no mean feat. Lifting the dead is a heavy burden, the living even more so. As David Ferry writes in a commentary on George Kalogeris' *Dialogos: Paired Poems in Translation*:

> The human quality that a good translation gives evidence of is generosity: the generosity of imagination that can hear and respond to the voice of somebody else which speaks or spoke in another language and place and sometimes time; the generosity that tries to reproduce, in so far as it can, the qualities of that voice, not only the data of what is said, but the feelings, the attitudes, the nuances, the shifts, the hesitations, the intensities, and the degrees of intensities, that he or she hears in that voice of somebody else.

Men and Sheep

SASKIA HAMILTON (trans.)

Men think that we here in the distance
are a flock of sheep – let them think,

we are not of a kind, we have no words
for ourselves, we still live in a time

when men too were sheep, and only
spoke grass, read light, wrote water.

RUTGER KOPLAND, 'Mens en schaap'

De mensen denken dat wij hier in de verte
een kudde schapen zijn – ze denken maar,

wij zijn niet eens wij, we hebben geen woorden
voor onszelf, we leven nog in de tijd hiervoor,

toen de mens nog schaap was, nog alleen
gras sprak, lucht las, water schreef.

'Not All the Confectionery': Michael Hofmann's Translations of German Novels

JAMES BUCHAN

Over the past thirty years, Michael Hofmann has translated nearly fifty works from German into English. Amid those translations, there is some verse, journalism and *feuilletonnerie*, a couple of books by and about the film director Wim Wenders, and two plays by Brecht.

His chief fame rests on translations of novels, stories and memoirs from the first half of the twentieth century, and novels by modern German, Austrian and Swiss authors who but for Hofmann would be unknown in the English-speaking lands that have all but given up learning the German language. Two of his translations, *The Land of Green Plums* (1998; *Herztier*) by the Romanian-German or *Banatschwäbin* Herta Müller, and Hans Fallada's *Alone in Berlin* (2009; *Jeder stirbt für sich allein*) have been bestsellers.

Once in Dresden a few years ago, under the pressure of flattery, Hofmann conceded that he had become 'a sort of defile' (*eine Art Engpass*) for writers in German. Those authors, toiling through the snow with their modal verbs and nouns substantive, crest a rise to glimpse in the sunshine below them the broad plain of English, teeming with readers and rich in money. For Anglo-American publishers, a book does not exist until it is in English and even Fallada's *Jeder stirbt*, which did well on its publication in 1946, was filmed for television in both wings of divided Germany and then again for the cinema in the west in 1975, had to be 'rediscovered' by Hofmann. Likewise Fred Wander's memoir of Buchenwald, *The Seventh Well* (2008; *Der siebente Brunnen*), was published in East Germany in 1971 but little known even in Jewish circles until Hofmann's translation.

The result is that in countries anxious about the future of German as a literary language, Hofmann has been garlanded with laurels. He has won the German Federal Republic's Schlegel-Tieck Prize twice and twice been runner-up. He has also been honoured by British and Irish benefactors.

Hofmann's success as a translator is unusual for two reasons. Since antiquity it has been the practice for a translator to render a text into his mother-tongue and not the other way round. Hofmann says he is German. Born in Freiburg im Breisgau in 1957, the son of refugees from the east, he came to England in 1961 when his father, Gert Hofmann, was sent as a university teaching assistant by the Federal German academic exchange programme (or DAAD) to Bristol. Michael Hofmann says he cannot remember learning English and that his 'first-ever British accent wavered / between Pakistani and Welsh' (*Acrimony*). He spoke German at home and his first reading was Karl May.

At the age of thirteen, Michael Hofmann won a scholarship to Winchester College, where he was immersed in the old-fashioned British public-school teaching of the dead languages. That education helped form not only his verse but his translations and is readily evident in his English style. For example, in his version of Kafka's *A Hunger Artist* (2007; *Ein Hungerkünstler*), there is no appearance of the word 'starvation', which to Latinists is a barbarism.

In 1971, the family split into three, his father moving to the university in Ljubjana in what was then Yugoslavia, his mother to Klagenfurt across the border in Austria, with Michael remaining in Winchester and then going up to Cambridge University. In the poems to and about Gert Hofmann in the second half of *Acrimony* (1986) and the first half of *Approximately Nowhere* (1999), Michael Hofmann reproduces snatches of his father's conversation in German. German is therefore not so much mother-tongue as father-tongue and his translations from German into English a sort of family reunion (or *Familienzusammen-*

führung, as it used to be called in the days before the Berlin Wall was demolished).

Michael Hofmann inhabits a world where language is a choice as it was for the Humanists such as Petrarch, du Bellay and Buchanan. His fluency in English and German is such that in certain of his translations, such as Wolfgang Koeppen's *Death in Rome* (1992; *Der Tod in Rom*), you feel you are reading a book by an Englishman but with thoughts no Englishman could possibly have entertained.

Secondly, Hofmann is the opposite of the journeyman translator who passes from one text to another as a pathologist to the next cadaver on the slab. He is a man of literary enthusiasm but also of literary antipathy, most notably for Stefan Zweig, all of von Hofmannstahl but *The Chandos Letter,* as well as Grass and Christa Wolf. He seems to have a low opinion of Böll or none at all. His preference is for the fiction and journalism of the 1920s and 1930s, or what he calls in his introduction to *Death in Rome* the 'silver age' of German literature. By that phrase (devised in the nineteenth century for the Latin authors of the later Roman Empire), he appears to mean that such writers as Kafka, Brecht, Roth and, at a pinch, Koeppen stand in the same relation to Goethe and Schiller as Juvenal to Horace. Kafka and Brecht probably needed none of Hofmann's assistance in Britain and the US but he has raised Joseph Roth, beginning with the *Legend of the Holy Drinker* (1989; *Die Legende vom heiligen Trinker*) to fame as the late historian or annalist of the Dual Monarchy. With Koeppen, whose three principal novels were published under the Federal Republic, he has been less successful and one wonders if *Death in Rome*, with its characters embodying supposed German vices like a Mystery Play or soap opera, is really as good as Hofmann says.

Yet within these likes and dislikes, Hofmann displays the professionalism of the repertory actor. It seemed to me, while I was reading the money-spinning *Alone in Berlin/Jeder stirbt*, that

Hofmann disliked Fallada (Rudolf Ditzen) both as a writer and as a man and was bored by the British love of all things National Socialist. A glance at the German text did nothing to soften that impression. Nonetheless, Hofmann gives the book the same attention as if it had been a work of Joseph Roth.

The modern novels he translates are as mixed a bag as one might find in English and French, but are never sold short. None of those translations gives an impression of difficulty or labour. None, as the eighteenth century used to say, 'smells of the lamp'. Standing in a special category are Hofmann's translations of the books his father wrote in the 1980s and 1990s: *Balzac's Horse* (1989; *Gespräch über Balzacs Pferd*), *The Film Explainer* (1995; *Der Kinoerzähler*) *Luck* (2002; *Das Glück*), *Lichtenberg and the Little Flower Girl* (2004; *Die kleine Stechardin*). In those translations, piety in the Virgilian sense of honouring one's parents must contend with all sorts of troublesome modern sensations. *Luck*, which tells of a father dismissed by his wife but unable to leave home, seemed to me heroic. Full of Kafka-ish stops and starts, it has this sentence: 'My sister had gone down into the garden to build an orphanage.'

For those wishing to emulate Hofmann's success, I can point to three of his strengths. The first is accuracy, by which I do not mean word-for-word translation – about which, more later – but a respect for profession or occupation whether in fact or fiction. There is no flinching or elision or bluff, whether the field be the cattle husbandry and butchery in Beat Sterchi's *Blösch* (1988) or the aerial munitions in Ernst Jünger's *Storm of Steel* (2003; *In Stahlgewittern*). In other words, if the German author knows what he is talking about (by no means guaranteed), then there will be no loss to the English reader and, perhaps, even, a small gain (about which, also, more later). He is hard on other translators' 'howlers' and is particularly withering about his predecessor with Jünger in the trenches, the prolific and long-lived Basil Creighton.

Secondly, Hofmann does not see it as his business to teach English speakers the German language or German history. Both word order and syntax are recast into good English. He is not much interested in German history, except as geography, and is entirely without that party-spirit that animates every section of Federal German society, even its police and armed forces. He has none of the British taste for the Third Reich or our expertise in its story. Thus in respect of the *Naziana* in Koeppen's *Death in Rome*, he writes in his introduction: 'I would like the English reader not to be too bothered by all this.' He continues: 'You feel the (foreign) texture of the word, take from the context whether it's a building or a political movement or a personality that's being referred to, and pass on.' Those are most un-German sentences.

That indifference or *sangfroid* is the key to his translation of Ernst Jünger's *In Stahlgewittern* (2003; *Storm of Steel*) and permits him to pass up the line without setting off all the un-exploded ordnance of national feeling and *antidemokratisches Denken* (anti-democratic thought) that make the book such an agony to readers in the modern Federal Republic. Using a text from 1978, Hofmann gives us none of the Fatherland-love and Tommy-killing that pervades Creighton's translation (or mangling, Hofmann would say) of the nationalist 1924 edition. Rather, Hofmann recognizes in, for example, Jünger's precise descriptions of fatal wounds and his lists of heroes the ghost of Homer's *Iliad* transposed to a *Materialschlacht* or artillery battle. In other words, Hofmann treats Jünger as a classical writer. In Hofmann's translation, there is no politics, no philosophy, no strategy and only platoon or small-company tactics. As he says in his introduction, 'the depth of focus of the book is maybe ten yards or so'. From Hofmann's translation, one would be hard pressed to say who, if anybody, had been victorious in the Great War of 1914–1918.

The third characteristic is a sort of immersion in his author which permits Hofmann, without in any way abolishing himself, to present a sort of essence or reduction of that author. It is the same translator that gives us the surly and half-deranged monologues of Thomas Bernhard's *Frost* (2006); the cartoonish flash and glitter of the opening of Roth's *The Radetzky March* (2002; *Radetzkymarsch*); and those sentences in Kafka that seem to be nothing more than a collection of German particles (*wenn, aber, da, nun, doch, auch*) and yet say things that nobody else has thought to say. Of those sentences, Hofmann writes in his introduction to *Metamorphosis and Other Stories* (2007): 'It's a hard thing to do what I've had to do here, to translate with an author and against a language.'

What is astonishing to me is that, without revealing a taste for war or any interest in military affairs, Hofmann gives us passages in *Storm of Steel* which appear to stand at the limit of what can be done with words in English. As Proust said of certain lines of Baudelaire, *il semble impossible d'aller au delà*. The fight at Guillemont during the Battle of the Somme is one of two or three high points in Hofmann's translations, another being the death of Gregor in Kafka's *Verwandlung* (*Metamorphosis and Other Stories*). Certain of Roth's less famous writings, which have come out under Hofmann's patronage, have been revelations. I am thinking, particularly, of the description of Roth's home town in Galicia. As I said, Hofmann is not much interested in history but he is in geography.

There seems to be, in Hofmann's art, something ineffable. Hofmann argues in a review of Edith Grossman's *Why Translation Matters* (2010): 'Translation for all that it seems a technical matter, is actually anything but. It's a mode of reading so sympathetic and transitive that the outcome is a wholly new work, it's hunch and nerve and (my own muse) impatience. It's approaching the avowed-impossible, and shrugging your shoulders and just getting on with it.' The passage reminded me of Borges' story, *Pierre Menard: Author of the Quixote*, in which a literary dandy sets out not to translate but to write *Don Quixote*: that is, learn Spanish to a high standard, recover his Catholic faith, fight against the Moors or the Turk, forget the history of Europe between 1602 and 1918, *be* Miguel de Cervantes. Once, when I asked Hofmann if he translated everything in Roth, he replied: 'Not all the confectionery.'

That has led to charges of inaccuracy. The most direct came in February 2002 in a review of Roth's *Collected Stories* in the *New York Review of Books,* where J. M. Coetzee accused Hofmann of 'improving' Roth or, at the very least, of abbreviating him. 'Is it part of a translator's job to give his author lessons in economy?' Coetzee asked. (Coetzee also, like a latter-day Dr Johnson, condemned Hofmann for the Scottishism 'haver'. He recommended a 'mid-Atlantic' dialect.) In his reply in the issue of 28 March, Hofmann wrote: 'Mr. Coetzee is wonderfully mistaken if he thinks a novel can be compared to an enormous number, and he can stand there and say, "There's an 8 – what have you done with it?" As someone who has written on Celan in your pages, Mr. Coetzee must know *really* that there are no exact equivalents anyway. *Brot* is not *bread*. Words are not like numbers, they are unstable and porous. A "word-for-word translation" is a rotten proposition: you'd get Gert Fröbe and not Joseph Roth.' (Gert Fröbe is the actor who played Goldfinger in *Goldfinger.*) He ends with a flourish: 'Last and least, I'm not British, I'm German.'

That can lead to a literary position so advanced that it is hard to imagine it can long be defended. In an essay on the aforesaid Celan, Hofmann approves the translation (by Felsinger) of the line from 'Todesfuge'

der Tod is ein Meister aus Deutschland

as

der Tod ist ein Meister aus Deutschland.

Hofmann asks in *Behind the Lines*: 'How can [. . .] "Deutsch-land" be rendered by the unfreighted and external "Germany" (with its distinct root of "Aleman-" for "Teutsch", all cosy and Western)?' No doubt, under the old principle of English juris-prudence that *hard cases make bad law*, it is rash to employ Celan as the starting- or end-point of any theory of translation. Actu-ally, I do not think Hofmann has a theory of translation.

More and more readers in the English-speaking countries now believe that works in German are just versions of Eng-lish literature that need to be straightened out. In reality, of course, German writing is not British, North American, Indian or Australian thoughts gone mysteriously awry but German thoughts in the only fashion they are intelligible. What, after all, is the purpose of learning a language if it is not to penetrate the thoughts expressed in it? It is ironic that by the excellence of his translations Hofmann merely confirms the English-speaking countries in their monoglot habit.

The Poet as Translator

SHAUN WHITESIDE

It's a truism to say that the translator walks a tightrope between the literal reading and the spirit of the original. Robert Lowell writes in the introduction to his wonderful but problematic *Imitations* – versions of poetry by Rilke, Rimbaud, Montale and others that 'the usual reliable translator gets the literal meaning but misses the tone, and [. . .] in poetry tone is of course everything.' In poetry of course it is, and in translation too, as Michael Hofmann – that rare thing, a star translator – knows, referring as he does to 'the translator who values voice in all writing'. A difficult one when the poet who is doing the translation has such a distinctive, sometimes daunting voice. We know it not only from his poetry, but from the criticism too, that steady glass-clear eye, the phrases that leap out and then linger in the mind – the enthusiasm for Lowell's 'fauve ooze' ('I lanced it in the fauve ooze for newts'), the 'sheepish punctilio' observed in the Swiss-German writer Robert Walser. A very meticulous, individual voice, one that it must be a stretch to restrain or disguise if the poet's voice is to become that of the translated author.

A valuable essay by the Belgian author Simon Leys on the work of translators who are themselves writers ('*La traduction*' in the collection *L'Ange et le cachalot*, 1998) suggests that translators are drawn to writers whose voices are somehow similar to, or complement, their own, just as a concert pianist might be drawn to the work of a particular composer for whom he has a particular affinity – Brendel and Beethoven, Gould and Bach, for example. A writer's translations, Leys says, are as much a part of his *oeuvre* as his own original works. In Michael Hofmann's case, there is a thread that pulls the oeuvre together. This is not the random ragbag of books that most translators are obliged to produce over a lifetime – the jumble of coming-of-age novels, thrillers, family sagas, psychoanalytical essays or historical tomes that allows us, in another of Hofmann's memorable phrases 'to scrape together a living in letters'. (I should perhaps declare an interest: my translation of Wim Wenders' essays, *Emotion Pictures*, an early effort on my part and no doubt crammed with rookie errors, was salvaged by Michael Hofmann and subsequently published under both our names.)

Michael Hofmann's body of translation constitutes a canon, and a fully coherent one alongside his own independent creations. Its milestones are perhaps too well known to recap, but they would include the rediscovery of Hans Fallada's *Jeder stirbt für sich allein*, translated as *Alone in Berlin*, a huge word-of-mouth success coming out of nowhere (and this is one instance in which the translator's name on the cover might well have boosted sales). The translation skilfully negotiates the demotic speech of 1930s Berlin, and in this instance, because style is not paramount, the translator vanishes discreetly behind the dark and vivid twists of the plot. This quick, dark tale contrasts with the vivid bleakness of *Herztier* (literally, 'Heartbeast') by Herta Müller, translated as *The Land of Green Plums*, a vivid, chilly piece set in Ceauşescu's Romania that creates music from tiny, concrete details. It won the Nobel for its author, and the IMPAC Prize for both. And then there are the novels of Michael's father Gert Hofmann, *Our Conquest*, *The Spectacle at the Tower* and *Das Glück*, translated as *Luck*. This is a study of marital breakdown as seen from the vantage point of a young boy, and the portrait of the father as a hopeless but supremely witty would-be novelist still hoping, in middle age, to emulate the success of Thomas Mann. Much of the humour lies in comic bluster, a mismatch, in this case, between everyday irritations and lofty discourse:

We lived, where we'd always lived, on the second floor

of 1 Jakobsstrasse. There were wood pigeons there.
They sat on our roof and shat on everything. My sister
would call to them: Coo coo coo! Come on, little baby
pigeons! Father would throw open a window and shout:
Begone monstrous brood!

Or:

But then Herr Schröder-Jahn wasn't coming after all,
he stopped at the kerb. Father waved to him a bit. If the
mountain won't go to Mohammed, then the Prophet
will just have to cross the street to the idiot on the other
side, he said under his breath.

A hapless reviewer in the *Times Literary Supplement* unwisely
took Hofmann to task for his translation of his father's novel and
particularly, as he saw it, for translating German idioms literally.
Hofmann responded: '. . . the shoes did go downstream. I was
four. They were my shoes.'

  Simon Leys refers to the ideal translating partnership as '*une
collaboration amoureuse*', and Hofmann has arguably found his in
what may be his towering achievement as a translator: the rediscovery and translation of the complete works of the Austrian
writer Joseph Roth. His introductions are a joy – the translator
is said to be a book's closest reader, and over the many volumes
of Roth's novels and journalism Hofmann has come to inhabit
his author. The most obvious cornerstone of the project might
be Roth's most celebrated novel, *The Radetzky March* (*Radetzkymarsch*), the collapse of the Austro-Hungarian Empire as seen by
three generations of the Trotta family, an astonishingly assured
and glittering performance. A sample from the novel's first page,
in German, then in a 1934 translation by Geoffrey Dunlop, and
then in Michael Hofmann's translation, may provide a clue as to
why Hofmann's was such a success:

Seit einer halben Stunde war das Gefecht im Gange. Drei Schritte vor sich sah er die weißen Rücken seiner Soldaten. Die erste Reihe seines Zuges kniete, die zweite stand. Heiter waren alle und sicher des Sieges. Sie hatten ausgiebig gegessen und Branntwein getrunken, auf Kosten und zu Ehren des Kaisers, der seit gestern im Felde war.

For half an hour the battle had been engaged. Three paces off before he watched the white backs of his men. Their first line was kneeling, the rear standing. They were all cheerful and sure of victory. They had eaten their bellyful and drunk brandy at the cost and in honour of their Emperor, who had been since yesterday in the field. (Dunlop)

The battle had been in progress for half an hour or so. Three paces in front of him, he saw the white-clad backs of his men. Their front line was down on one knee, their second stood. They had had a good meal and drunk brandy in honour and at the expense of their Emperor, who had been present on the field of battle since yesterday. (Hofmann)

There is an easy fluency here – as indeed there is in Hofmann's marvellous translations from Kafka – that draws the reader in, that illuminates details and carries the narrative vividly, almost cinematically along, a tweaking of details and tenses – 'white-clad backs', 'their second stood' – brings the images uncannily to life.

Unexpectedly, though, I think the crowning glory of the Roth series may not be so much the novels, wonderful as they are, but the correspondence as recorded in *Joseph Roth: A Life in Letters*. In this volume, Michael Hofmann manages to maintain the voice of Joseph Roth as he progresses from the cockiness of youth to the anger and irritability of the mature author and journalist, to the anxiety and ultimately resignation of the man who knows he isn't going to live beyond middle age. At the heart of the book is the correspondence between the often chaotic Roth and his friend Stefan Zweig, sympathetically conveyed throughout, despite Hofmann's well-known antipathy towards the literary elder statesman. The Roth translations are indispensable, but the correspondence is a tour de force.

I hope Anthea Bell won't mind me quoting her as describing Michael Hofmann 'a peerless translator of poetry'. In his essential *Faber Book of 20th-Century German Poems*, he introduces this sinewy, intelligent tradition based around Brecht ('seid Sand, nicht Öl, im Getriebe der Welt': 'be sand, not oil, in the machinery of the world'), Gottfried Benn, Günter Eich and Paul Celan, with Durs Grünbein taking us into the present day. Sadly for the Germanist, the anthology contains no poems in the original, but it does contain some great translations by an array of carefully chosen translators. The emphasis is more, perhaps, on Brecht's stripped-down anti-rhetoric than on Rilke's ecstatic visions. I suspect Rilke's music doesn't greatly appeal to Michael Hofmann, but Gottfried Benn's 'Nachtcafé' ('Night Café') plainly does:

824: Der Frauen Liebe und Leben.
Das Cello trinkt nach mal. Die Flöte
Rülpst tief drei Takte lang: das schöne Abendbrot.
Die Trommel liest den Kriminalroman zu Ende.

Grüne Zähne, Pickel im Gesicht
Winkt einer Lidrandentzündung.

Fett im Haar
Spricht zu offenem Mund mit Rachenmandel
Glaube Liebe Hoffnung um den Hals.

And in Michael Hofmann's translation:

> 824: Lives and Loves of Women.
> The cello takes a quick drink. The flute
> Belches expansively for three beats: good old dinner.
> The timpani is desperate to get to the end of his thriller
>
> Mossed teeth and pimple face
> Wave to incipient stye.
>
> Greasy hair
> Talks to open mouth with adenoids
> Faith Love Hope round her neck.

The synecdoches are grim and funny – I'm not sure that until reading Hofmann's version I'd noticed just how gruesomely funny they are. Benn was a doctor, of course, and each observation here is a diagnosis, the eye unable or unwilling to look away. The forensic approach is even more apparent in Benn's poem 'Kleine Aster' ('Little Aster'), from the 'Morgue' sequence.

> Ein ersoffener Bierfahrer wurde auf den Tisch gestemmt.
> Irgendeiner hatte ihm eine dunkelhellila Aster
> Zwischen die Zähne geklemmt.
> Als ich von der Brust aus
> unter der Haut
> mit einem langen Messer
> Zunge und Gaumen herausschnitt,
> muß ich sie angestoßen haben, den sie glitt
> in das nebenliegende Gehirn.

And in Michael Hofmann's translation:

A drowned truck-driver was propped on the slab.
Someone had stuck a lavender aster
between his teeth.
As I cut out the tongue and the palate,
through the chest
under the skin,
with my long knife,
I must have touched the flower, for it slid
into the brain lying next.

Poetic freedoms have been taken – the dark-bright-purple ('dunkelhellila') aster is now a less convoluted 'lavender', the knife's trajectory moves up the page rather than down, but still the poem is itself: a dissector's eye, a startling juxtaposition, a flower in a drayman's brain.

Again, affinity (Verwandschaft) is key and there are poets in the Faber anthology – Bartsch, Sielaff – who seem as if they might have learned from Hofmann's own poetic practice. Diction is unadorned, bold ideas sparked by everyday objects. From Volker Sielaff's 'Creation Myth':

She takes a Kleenex
and wipes herself. The following gesture
is already borrowed and pre-programmed.

They were
certainly not tired, that much
should be understood. Maybe he just
stretched out beside her, under

the apple tree, or he went
looking for a cigarette, it's natural
to feel a little bit sad afterwards,
isn't that right?

That's Sielaff's use of the proprietary brand, by the way, not Hofmann's: the colloquial tone belongs to them both. But it's with the poet Durs Grünbein that the great affinity – the ideal relationship between author and translator, what Leys rather Frenchly calls, as I mentioned earlier, a *'collaboration amoureuse'*. This collaboration is emphatically not French in tone, but is the happiest imaginable encounter between poet and translator. Grünbein's poems are both lexically dense and colloquial, intellectual, often surreal and wryly funny. Like Michael Hofmann's own poems, they take imagery from the everyday and spark it into poetic life. The collection *Ashes for Breakfast* was rightly awarded the Oxford-Weidenfeld Prize. Below, a poem from *Nach den Satiren* (1999).

(Von den Tageszeitungen)

Ich habe Asche gegessen zum Frühstück, den schwarzen
Staub, der aus Zeitungen fällt, aus den druckfrischen
    Spalten,
Woe in Putsch keine Flecken macht und der Wirbel-
    sturm steht.
Und es schien mir, als schmatzten sie, die parlierenden
    Parzen,

Wenn im Sportteil der Krieg began, dem der Ak-
    tienkurs traut.
Ich habe Asche gegessen zum Frühstück. Meine Tages-
    diät.
Und von Clio, wie immer, kein Sterbenswort . . . Da,
    beim Falten,
Lief das Rascheln der Seiten als Schauer mir über die
    Haut.

(On the Daily Newspapers)

I have breakfasted on ashes, the black
Dust that comes off newspapers, from the freshly
    printed colums.
When a coup makes no stain, and a tornado sticks to
    half a page.
And it seemed to me as though the Fates licked their lips

When war broke out in the sports section, reflected in
    the falling Dow.
I have breakfasted on ashes. My daily bread.
And Clio, as ever, keeps mum . . . There, just as I folded
    them up,
The rustling pages sent a shiver down my spine.

In his *TLS* letter about his father's novel *Luck*, Michael Hofmann spoke of the 'pathetic prospects for German literature in
English'. That was only eight years ago, but it seems a lifetime
away, not least thanks to the tireless work of Hofmann himself
in bringing German writing back into the mainstream. He is
not alone, of course – Anthea Bell, for example, has done a huge
amount to keep German writing in the public eye – but his gifts
as a poet and his intense critical appreciation of nearly forgotten
works of the past give him a special status that the rest of us can
only dream of.

The Courtesan

CHRISTOPHER REID

after Rainer Maria Rilke

The sun of Venice
will refine my hair
to gold: all alchemy's
glorious outcome.
My brows are like
her bridges: look
how they arch the silence
and menace of my eyes,
which have entered into
a secret alliance
with her canals,
so the sea itself
surges, ebbs
and throbs in them.
Whoever's seen me
once at once
resents my lap-dog,
with which, in fits
of absentmindedness,
my hand, which no heat
has ever touched,
but which is invulnerable
and bejewelled,
will toy. And boys,
the scions of dynasties,
perish from my kisses,
as if poisoned.

Bowled Over

'The anti-aircraft guns threaded long fleecy lines through the air, and whistling splinters pinged into the tilth.'

This is from Michael Hofmann's translation of *Storm of Steel*, by Ernst Jünger. '. . . whistling splinters pinged into the tilth' – this wonderfully jumpy variation on an iambic pentameter line I take as a personal message from Michael to me, and to any other poet who might happen to read the book. I concede the phrase might be a literal translation of the original, but I prefer to think it's Michael doing a little poetry dance for us, his secret sharers.

Thank you, Michael.

Now here's a passage from one of Michael's own poems, 'On the Beach at Thorpeness.'

> Roaring waves of fighters head back to Bentwaters.
> The tide advanced in blunt cod's-head curves,
> ebbed through the chattering teeth of the pebbles.
> Jaw jaw. War war.

That's Michael spinning his own intricate music. I'll thank him for that, too, and for all the other musically deft and delicate lines he's devised, and all the dense, moving poems, whose stanzas he himself well described as 'bricks': hard, uncompressible, precise, no slops of mortar hanging out of the joints.

I love Michael Hofmann's poetry, and have for a long time. I admire enormously and am grateful for his translations, especially his indispensible versions of Durs Grünbein. He also often awes me in his thinking and writing about poetry, which he does on a level nearly no one else approaches.

One of the saddest truths of being a poet, being in the poetry world, living the poetry life, is that so much of the sparse volume of serious commentary on poetry is so, to be frank, lame. Lame, off the point, inept, and, worst, seemingly oblivious to the real purposes of poetry, and the real concerns of poets making and/or trying to make poems.

The first essay of Michael's I ever experienced I heard him deliver aloud at a poetry festival somewhere in the UK. It was on Lowell: I was, really, almost literally, bowled over. I'd never heard such a wise, sane, grown-up consideration of Lowell, his life, his work. I was taken with sheer delight: so much about Lowell had been cast in a new, calm, intense, probing light, that amplified, for me, Lowell's work, which had been trivialized by so much of the glop that had been written about him.

Ever since, I've always been thrilled to see that some prose by Michael was appearing in an issue of *Poetry*, or anywhere else. He's had a continuing adventure with Lowell, and one of his most insightful essays has to do with Lowell and Bishop, their friendship, their nearly celestial (but always very human) near spiritual fusions, and the mostly unacknowledged competitiveness on Lowell's part. Who but Michael would entitle such an essay 'The Linebacker and the Dervish'? And who else, into a stunning comment on one of Lowell's poems ('The Restoration') and his differences from Bishop, could come up with something as precise and wild as: 'This is the poet as house plant, as aspirin-munching studio beast, a day-for-night alice band. Lowell is the linebacker-turned-pasha as poet, Bishop is the lifelong dervish.'

From *Poetry*, too, came Hofmann on Fred Seidel, surely the most misunderstood and misread of contemporary poets, whose work Michael manages to analyze and exalt and find schemes for speaking of the poems in a way that both acknowledges their often strange shticks and illuminates their quite astonishing originality and skill.

Before I close, I should also say I find Michael as a person to be particularly sympathetic, warm, unpretentious, and attractively and enviably taciturn. He simply does not suffer himself to be a fool, even for a moment, and I find this quite wonderful, so different from the way I am myself, often filling the air with blab, then having to spend much time and effort rectifying.

I once happened to chair a panel on translation at a poetry festival at Princeton on which Michael was a participant. There was no particular aspect of translation we'd been instructed to discuss, no angle of approach to take – we were really just winging it. 'We' being Michael, Durs Grünbein, Galway Kinnell, Ellen Doré Watson, and me, the presumed moderator. I thought I'd begin the proceedings by asking Michael to make a little statement on his vast experiences as a translator, so I looked down the table to where he was sitting at the other end, and said something to that effect.

Michael looked at me silently, with no expression I could name, but with a scrutiny that seemed to be asking me what in heaven's name I might mean by asking such a rather empty question. We looked at each other for a long moment, and I realized that Michael was not going to start up the engine of his thought unless I could come up with a query that would have something more than a merely conventional substance, and finally I turned to Galway instead and directed at him a more specific question about certain disagreements he and I have had over the years about translation. The audience laughed, with appreciation for Michael, I like to think, and perhaps with a similar affection to what I myself felt right then for him, his unwavering integrity, his bullshit sensor.

Admirable artist, admirable man.

Hofmannesque

GEORGE SZIRTES

1

Almost a clicking of heels: he smiles, bows
and flickers. His eyes freeze then burn a little.
The courtly manners of loss at an edge.
Tact and fury and the rain outside
that seems as though it might go on for ever.

2

He does the police and every other voice
in as clear a fashion as the dream permits.
The menu is brought in, painfully, by a waiter
who attends on worlds in the process of vanishing.
The hours are long, the routine punishing.

3

So much the poem offers itself
to fortune, is cast adrift yet stays afloat.
The clear cut, the carving in the bone
of language that sticks, like love, in the throat.

4

The translator is always on the edge of becoming,
but it is someone else he or she becomes.
The disasters of war are set to work in the kitchen
while the dead twiddle their thumbs.

5

If this were the old empire I'd invite you to Budapest
to sort out the natives. One aristocratic glance
of your poet's eye would keep the thugs in their station
muttering curses at you, prince.

Who needs a throne when they can write
    commandments?

Painting Michael Hofmann

ARTURO DI STEFANO

When it was proposed that I make a portrait of Michael Hofmann I would have preferred, ideally, to paint him from life but realized this wouldn't be feasible due to his teaching commitments in Florida and his living in Hamburg during semester breaks. However, there are more ways of capturing a likeness than holding someone captive in the studio for hours on end. His absence from London over the years has been punctuated by the regular appearances of his translations of both prose and poetry, as well as essays and articles in the press and literary magazines. Wherever he was in the world it was obvious he was working and producing stuff at a prodigious rate. My only concern was that the photograph used in his *Guardian* by-line didn't quite resemble the Michael I knew; it seemed as if an approximate look-alike had been hired as a stand-in to cover for him. It was reassuring, therefore, to see him at the Jewish Book Week in February 2012 looking his familiar self, older of course, hair slightly grey, the eyes a little more deep-set with the look of a heavy reader, though they still flashed and widened in response to some private thought or observation. I'd gone on spec, having read his *Guardian* article by chance the day before, which gave details of the talk on his latest Joseph Roth book: *A Life in Letters*. It was fortunate I had taken a camera along because I later learned that this was a flying visit and that he wouldn't be back in England for about a year. It was with a sense of urgency, therefore, that after the talk, coffee and chit-chat, I suggested we made use of the quickly fading afternoon light to take some shots as this was the only opportunity to have any evidential record to work from, if you excluded some hastily written notes

I made during and shortly after our impromptu meeting. A few months later I began the painting.

I'd had the prepared canvas for a long time, waiting for an appropriate subject. I knew its luminous white half-chalk ground would make any colour applied to it sing. From the dozen or so photos I had taken only one proved suitable for the image I had in mind – frontal, looking directly at the viewer, the face recognizably his, without the rigid self-consciousness of being posed.

During the making of a painting a spell is cast in which thoughts and memories arise unbidden so that contemplation of the immediate task at hand – mixing colours, making decisions where and how to apply them and so on – is joined by a parallel reverie of previous shared experiences between subject and painter that becomes part of the act and is transmuted by paint into the image. I don't say this is deliberate or planned beforehand – it either happens or it doesn't – but I think it's an event that determines the degree to which a painting is deemed successful, and is something that can't be expressed directly but disclosed by hints and glimpses. What *can* be talked about is the choice of background colour (three colours in fact: yellow ochre overlaid by a film of cadmium yellow and over that a yellow ochre pale) and its pictorial function as a complementary colour to offset the flesh tones and to balance the cobalt green and ultramarine of the shirt and cardigan. Another thing I was most certainly conscious of was Michael's poetry, especially the line 'All things tend towards the yellow of unlove', and how it evoked other ideas and moments: the radiance of Van Gogh's *Sunflowers*, for instance, which explores and exploits the full gamut of yellow, from lemon to ochre; the setting sun's autumnal golden light illuminating the buildings and water in King's Place, where we met after too long an absence. He and his poetry, and this line in particular, made me try harder for the image of him to count and for its yellow to be taken as tending towards a form of love.

Hofmann on Hofmann

LAWRENCE JOSEPH

'I was pushing twenty-two. It was May or June of 1979, and it was the year, maybe the month I was graduating – in absentia, what else. Some people I knew were putting on a poetry festival in Cambridge, and I went along to some of the events in the big old Corn Exchange, where the Clash had played, and Richard Hell. My relationship with poetry was that I scorned it, and felt sorry for it. I actually meant words at all times, I didn't want to be a rock star or a comedian, but poetry as it seemed to propose itself to me – or to me then – was awful. A type of crippled language that couldn't say what it meant, that was always – like Cambridge, like England – nostalgic for better times, a hopeless anachronism, little better than lavender spats. And yet it was what I was trying to write – fiction had defeated me – and, where possible, to read. I had known poets before, had had an English teacher who was one, and a geography teacher; at school older boys had worn their ties 'at half-mast' when Pound died and Auden died, but probably this was my first veritable experience of poets. I don't think my expectations were keyed up. I wasn't cynical so much as unhopeful. Into this abeyance marched – well, several people, but most particularly Hans Magnus Enzensberger, who sounds like several people anyway, and certainly does the work of several people.'

'Into the Abeyance', *Poetry*, July/August 2008

'"Most days," I once wrote, "I neither read nor write." It's still true. If not more so. I keep no notebooks, no dream journal, I have no ideas for poems, no sheaf of half-written drafts. A peculiar sort of life, really. The opposite of ergonomic or diligent. Imagine a pilot who doesn't fly, a salesman who clinches no deals, a gambler who stands in front of a fruit machine, with his few thin dimes, waiting for the moment.'

'Sing Softer: A Notebook', *Poetry*, September 2005

'One has one's pantheon, and one seeks gently to extend it. You need to read to write. (That was my advice one year to students, read and walk. And I would leave it up to them to do their own walking.) Further, you need to change what you read to change what you write. You're like a spider, rigging your net among what you take to be fixed points, and gradually bringing in new ones. I'm not bored with my pantheon ('Circumspice!'), and I don't think I've anywhere near exhausted it, but for a long time I've thought my failure to write more has stemmed from my failure to read – I mean really: read and endorse, or read-some-one-in-the-sense-of-wanting-to-write-them, read as an owlish vulture might read – more.'

'Sing Softer: A Notebook', *Poetry*, September 2005

'One exists in a tightening spiral of one's aging likes. Perhaps it's even a little worse than that, because these things, in some sense, are not even outside oneself any more in any meaningful way. That's the strange thing about this reinforcing rereading one does; you read things again and again, even though you know perfectly well how they go, what comes next, what they mean. It's more a kind of compacting or mulching, an endless apply-ing of some substance that you have selected for osmosis – if it hasn't found *you*. The removal of any residual barriers between yourself and your preferred or designated verbal matter. I think I now understand why in his later years my father, the novel-ist Gert Hofmann, didn't read, but only reread, even though at the time it seemed utterly stultifying to me: Bernhard, Mann, Kafka, Faulkner – this last even in German translation, for rea-sons I still don't understand.'

'Sing Softer: A Notebook', *Poetry*, September 2005

'Somehow, quite without my realizing it, I seem to have spent half my life with Benn; in his centenary year, 1986, I reviewed the two-volume edition of his poems and Holthusen's biography of him. He has influenced me, not only to translate him in the first place, but also *while not* translating him. Over the years, thanks in part to Benn, my own sentences have become more indeterminate, my language more musical, my diction more – no pun intended – florid. There is a sort of murmurous, *mi-voix*, *halblaut* quality in poems that I adore, and – languidly – strive for. I was all the time quietly being readied for a task I hardly dared suppose I would ever take on.'

'Threat: Translator's Note', *Poetry*, March 2011

'To return to the poems here, though, I realize that they are what I always had in mind in my long-held desire for, and appreciation of, what I termed "old man poems." Instead of the discipline of music and meter, they have the discipline of speech . . . That "fascination" that Benn identified as the elusive but irreducible quality of poetry inheres in them as much as it does in the rhyming strophes; effectively, both are collages of the most varied and spirited diction. The growly misanthropic cuss who speaks them is as much an invention and a function of style as the brittle and glitteringly impersonal manner of the octaves. Though light, they are wonderfully heavy with experience, "a pile of life in variegated forms." For me translating them is something like having evolved, over time, a personality or character, and then being told there is just such a character, and being asked to play it: an unintended variant on "method" acting. I loved these poems when I first read and wrote about them twenty years ago; yet somehow – youth? trepidation? selfish possession rather than working to make them available to an English readership? – I never allowed myself to think I might actually translate them.'

'Notorious Ever After: A Note on Benn', *Poetry*, October 2006

'Poetry is – as the poet said, though his subject was butterflies – an army of stragglers. Contemporaries, aeons, and cultures apart slog wordlessly through the mud together, not at all pally, not at all like Virgil and Dante. There's no uniform, no team shirt, no battle or plan of battle, no weapons, no organization, no hierarchy, no ranks or badges except for homemade ones that don't count, enemies and detractors everywhere. Its colors you should think twice before rallying around (I don't know what they are, perhaps sable on sable), and its only cavalry is the reader, and there's only one of him or her, sitting at home minding his or her own business, without a horse to hand, or a thought of you. There are plenty of fellow travellers, whom you can tell from their air of confidence and impunity, and because they tend to get there faster. (Even though of course there is no 'there'.) – How can I call anyone to the barricades?'

'Manifesto of the Flying Mallet', *Poetry*, February 2009

'Twelve years ago I took a half-time appointment teaching poetry in Florida among the alligators and the babeage. I was tired of the attrition of having to write/review/translate for a living. I thought it might move poetry a little closer to the center of things for me. (It has done, but it's the poetry of students; one is paid, I think pessimistically, not to write. No wonder so many American poems have "vacation" written all over them, "part-time sublime," "cultural tourism," or "occasional wilderness fix." And it's not just America any more either. Britain and Germany, and no doubt others, are following suit.) Little wonder, maybe, that one persuades oneself that the noblest thing one can do is not to contribute to the poetry glut. *Non servam.* I have no words for my predicament. If I was an actor, I could at least say, "I'm resting."'

'Sing Softer: A Notebook', *Poetry*, September 2005

'I am hostile to the very idea of poetry, so to speak, in the plural, as a collective mass or enterprise. Poetry as a certain good. The laureates in this country and in England are busy promulgating something I wouldn't care to promulgate myself. (The key word is "busy" – I see them as the lovely and untranslatable German phrase, "*Hans Dampf in allen Gassen*," "Hans making steam in all the alleyways": busybodies.) If someone gave me (though "I prefer not") the platform of a poetry column, I think I could keep it up for about six weeks. And then "That's all, folks," and the Woody Woodpecker laugh. There is room in the world for bad or middling novels, but somehow not for bad poems. Perhaps because, as I think Les Murray says somewhere, "we are a language species," and really the only thing one can do for oneself amidst the proliferation of language – especially English! – is to keep a little parcel of it reasonably pure or controlled in one's own mind. And if that sounds too tame and restrictive, even people who like jungles keep gardens.'

'Sing Softer: A Notebook', *Poetry*, September 2005

'For upwards of twenty-five years, you have written English poems, and translated not poetry, but German prose. You felt no particular disquiet at this separation of powers. But finally, you don't want to spend your entire life in avoidance of something, in fear or disdain, however well grounded. There are translations of foreign poets to which you feel deep gratitude: Cavafy, Akhmatova, Zagajewski, Montale. You love your Waley and your Pound. In fact, the first poet you ever read, at the age of eight, was in translation: Zbigniew Herbert. (The poem was "From Antiquity," the one about the barbarians and the little salt god, and you've never forgotten it.) Above all, you feel an attachment to the idea that you have some German poet twin – the one who, unlike you, stayed at home – whom it is your duty and your sacred pleasure to translate into English.'

'Translator's Preface', *Ashes for Breakfast: Selected Poems*, Durs Grünbein

'I expected to translate a novel a year, or every other year, to stay busy, and to make a little money. It's rather run away with me. I've even lost count of how many books I've done. I suppose Joseph Roth is the main culprit (I'm working on my tenth book of his, an annotated selection of his letters), but there are others too whom I couldn't stand not to do: Wolfgang Koeppen (four titles), Wim Wenders (three), my father (three again). I'm translating my second Kafka (the short stories), my second Brecht (*Mother Courage*). I don't really know what it is. An expression of my fealty to German? Or to prose? Something Machiavellian, a practical identification of a type of work that's always there to do, and that's endlessly portable? Or something altogether more sinister: a kind of driven self-obliteration? Am I pushing myself forward, or holding myself back? I dislike the process and the work, but I love the results, the finished books.'

Interview with Mark Thwaite, 2005'

'None of the books I have translated have given me more pleasure than *The Hothouse* and *Death in Rome*. I find Koeppen's "hammernder Sprechstil," as it was described by one critic, his "hammering parlando," completely congenial. I love the way he hides a phrase on a page, and a scene in a book; it takes many readings to become aware of the richness and the breadth of his vision, of his prismatic way with details and motifs. His rhetorical approach to a sentence, improvising and appositional, but wound tight in a mighty rhythm, is quite exhilarating. (You need to read them "aloud" to yourself.)'

'Introduction' to *The Hothouse* by Wolfgang Koeppen

'Who had the best poets in the twentieth century? For their size of population, the Irish and the Poles, absolutely, without hesitation. And under open rules? Well, then it's more like the usual suspects, the Americans and the Russians, the Spanish (particularly if you throw in Latin America) and (beefed up by the Austrians and the Swiss, and a few Czechs and Balts and Romanians) the Germans. I don't think I'm being biased here, except inasmuch as I am able to read the stuff at all. If you're a monoglot in English, you have to struggle mightily to make your Mercator look any better adjusted or more adequately representative than the famous *New Yorker* map of the States. ("Do you mean *foreign* poetry?" exclaims a coiled, repugnant Larkin, asked if he read poetry in translation. As if English poetry in (English!) translation might be acceptable.) To answer the question fairly and properly, you'd have to be a thoroughgoing polyglot; and I'm only a bi-glot.'

'Introduction' to *Twentieth-Century German Poetry: An Anthology*

'To my mind, Lowell put words together as compellingly as anyone in English in the twentieth century; along with Benn and Montale, he is one of its great voices: like them, he understood that the modern poem is all about vocal quality, "*monologisch*" in Benn's word. He applied Pound's invention, logopoeia, to a prose diction, and wrote lines – when he had a mind to – as mighty as Marlowe's.'

'Introduction' to *Robert Lowell: Poems Selected by Michael Hofmann*

'It was reading Robert Lowell that brought me to poetry at the age of 19, in 1976. I had borrowed a friend's omnibus edition of *Life Studies* and *For the Union Dead*, and something in me said: "This is it!" . . . Twenty-seven years later, I'm afraid I haven't got beyond that initial feeling; I signed up to do a PhD on Lowell, which remained unwritten because there was never anything I wanted to prove about him. I didn't have a "thesis", in any sense. I still don't. Instead, Lowell is someone I continually reread. I find his poems endlessly approachable, wonderfully communicative and perfectly inexhaustible: stately, supple, personal and resourceful. To vary what Mallarmé says about himself (Lowell quotes it in his last book, *Day by Day*), here was someone who had the good fortune to find a style that made writing possible. By comparison with him, other poets don't use language, don't write about the world.'

'His Own Prophet', *London Review of Books*, Vol. 25, 11 Sept. 2003

'I treasure my battered copy of *Notebook*, with its sticker "5 fl. dump special" – I bought it in Amsterdam some time in the 1980s. I should have bought half a dozen of them, shoaled like Gong albums or old soaps after Christmas in a chemist's.'

'His Own Prophet', *London Review of Books*, Vol. 25, 11 Sept. 2003

'I read and admire Schuyler with the same part of me that reads and admires Lowell. To make sense of "The Payne Whitney Poems", I contend that it helps to have read "For Sale", "Waking in the Blue", "The Mouth of the Hudson", "Myopia: A Night", perhaps even "Waking Early Sunday Morning". Yes, Schuyler has a different register, his words emerge either slower or faster than Lowell's, more sparingly or more drenchingly (in "Arches", it is slow and spare), but both are in the same business of forging a written voice or making print that sounds. It doesn't seem to me justifiable to set the author of "I keep no rank nor station. / Cured, I am frizzled, stale and small" against the author of "Arches" – besides, Elizabeth Bishop was a great admirer of both.'

'Slowly/Swiftly', *London Review of Books*, Vol. 24, 7 Feb. 2002

'Quoting is very much to the point. I have gravitated to the longer pieces, not so that I can the more effectively overwhelm you, as the wolf might have said to Little Red Riding Hood, but if anything for the opposite reason: to allow me to supply more context, more information, more quotation, so that what I write becomes something more than the transmission of an opinion. I am not chary of opinions, and have at least as much faith in my own as the next person, but if this is to amount to anything as a book, I will have to do a little more than give points out of ten.'

'Introduction' to *Behind the Lines*

'I like detail, and I like bold outlines. I like to know something about the people I read. Among other things, I was interested in getting an education. Reviewing stretched me and consumed me as much as poetry did. It was as a reviewer that I first read Roth and Celan and Trakl; that I saw Wenders making ever dodgier films while (in the books of his I was translating at the same time) talking better and better ones; that I got my first proper sight of Kiefer; that gave me a chance to pay my respects to O'Hara, to Musil, to Brodsky, to Konwicki.'

'Introduction' to *Behind the Lines*

'Translation is a subject that empties rooms probably faster than poetry, which is supposed to have that effect. I am sorry to raise it. The imputation that I go around "making Roth better" I regard as a slur, and reject. Mr. Coetzee is wonderfully mistaken if he thinks a novel can be compared to an enormous number, and he can stand there and say, "There's an 8 – what have you done with it?" As someone who has written on Celan in your pages, Mr. Coetzee must know *really* that there are no exact equivalents anyway. *Brot* is not *bread*. Words are not like numbers, they are unstable and porous. A "word-for-word translation" is a rotten proposition: you'd get Gert Frobe and not Joseph Roth. The things in my translation that Mr. Coetzee took issue with, I would probably do the same way again. Each of his instances – what of, exactly? – are matters of degree. It is my sense of English that it would rather "flea-spotted" than an adjectival phrase (it doesn't offer the agreements of German); "burnished" rather than something involving a change of subject and a reflexive verb (but it has a larger vocabulary). English is generally shorter and faster and less given to elaborate structures. Translations of German books into English are known to be a tenth to a fifth shorter; translations into German, as much longer. It's not just me doing it . . . On the matter, lastly, of mid-Atlantic, I don't think my editor at Norton, Robert Weil, would ever let me get too British. Secondly, it is something I am in a position consciously to vary; I do tend to think British English, even for American readers, may be more appropriate for older Continental writing. (This is not, please note, a "platform" or "position," merely the result of doing and thinking about these things for a number of years.) I have made some mid-Atlantic translations; even some that I flattered myself were largely American. Last and least, I'm not British, I'm German.'

'Letter to the Editors', *New York Review of Books*, 28 March 2002

'You see, of the various fields I peruse here, American poetry, European poetry, painting, stage and screen, prose fiction, I am not really entitled to any of them. None of them are "mine". Wherever I go, I find myself treading on other people's turf, if not toes. Much more, I tend to think, disqualifies me than qualifies me: I am not British, I am not American, I am not a novelist, never raised a brush, never studied German. Nor do I make any appeal to my authority – if any – as a poet. I am not interested in producing a sort of Arcimboldo self-portrait made of book reviews, I write as a reader and observer, and if I have any authority it is the nervous authority of the reader.'

'Introduction' to *Behind the Lines*

'With the appearance of *Rebellion*, we now have all of Joseph Roth's completed novels, fifteen of them, in English translation, sixty years after his death. It has taken a dozen translators and a score of publishing houses, in Britain and America, but the intermittent, idealistic, and determined enterprise is complete, and a classic accolade has been assembled for a classic writer.

One might think of a relay race – one in which the baton is neglected for the best part of forty *years* between the thirties and the seventies – or the efforts of a willing, if amateurish, team of skittles players. Briefly atop this heap of literary coral, I feel a modicum of triumph, a degree of shame, and a strong sense of being at a loss. *"Und dann? Und dann?"* as my father would sometimes say, "What next? What next?'"

'Joseph Roth', in *Behind the Lines*

Awards & Bibliography

Awards

Thornton Wilder Prize (2012)
Jewish Quarterly Wingate Prize (2009)
Oxford-Weidenfeld Translation Prize (2007)
Mildred L. Batchelder Award (2006)
Oxford-Weidenfeld Translation Prize (2004)
Helen and Kurt Wolff Translator's Prize (2000)
PEN/Book-of-the-Month Club Translation Prize (1999)
International IMPAC Dublin Literary Award (1998)
Arts Council Writers' Award (1997)
Independent Foreign Fiction Prize (1995)
Schlegel-Tieck Prize (1993)
Schlegel-Tieck Prize (1988)
Geoffrey Faber Memorial Prize (1986)
Cholmondeley Award (1984)

Poetry

Nights in the Iron Hotel (Faber, 1983)
Acrimony (Faber, 1986)
K.S. in Lakeland: New and Selected Poems (Ecco Press, 1990)
Corona, Corona (Faber, 1993)
Approximately Nowhere (Faber, 1999)
Selected Poems (Faber, 2008; FSG, 2009)

Criticism

Behind the Lines (Faber, 2001)
Where Have You Been? (FSG, 2014)

As Editor

After Ovid: New Metamorphoses (with James Lasdun; Faber, 1994)
Selected Poems of Robert Lowell (Faber, 2001)
Selected Poems of John Berryman (Faber, 2004)
The Faber Book of 20th Century German Poems (Faber, 2005; US
    bilingual edition, *Twentieth-Century German Poetry: An
    Anthology*, FSG, 2008)
The Voyage That Never Ends: Michael Lowry in His Own Words
    (NYRB, 2007)
Joseph Roth: A Life in Letters (Granta, 2012; W. W. Norton,
    2012)

Translations: Poetry

Ashes for Breakfast: Selected Poems, Durs Grünbein (Faber, 2005)
Angina Days: Selected Poems, Günter Eich (Princeton, 2010)
Impromptus: Selected Poems and Some Prose, Gottfried Benn
    (FSG, 2013; Faber, 2013)

Translations: Prose

Castle Gripsholm, Kurt Tucholsky (Chatto & Windus, 1985)
The Double Bass, Patrick Süskind (Hamish Hamilton/Penguin,
    1987)
Blösch, Beat Sterchi (Faber, 1988)
Balzac's Horse and Other Stories, Gert Hofmann (with
    Christopher Middleton; Secker & Warburg, 1989)
Emotion Pictures, Wim Wenders (with Shaun Whiteside; Faber,
    1989)
The Good Person of Sichuan, Bertolt Brecht (Methuen, 1989)
The Legend of the Holy Drinker, Joseph Roth (Chatto, 1989;
    Overlook, 1995)
Right and Left, Joseph Roth (Chatto, 1991; Overlook, 2004)
Death in Rome, Wolfgang Koeppen (Hamish Hamilton/
    Penguin, 1991; W. W. Norton, 2001)

The Logic of Images, Wim Wenders (Faber, 1991)

The Story of Mr Sommer, Patrick Süskind (Bloosmbury, 1992)

The Lord Chandos Letter, Hugo Von Hofmannsthal (Penguin, 1995)

The Film Explainer, Gert Hofmann (Secker & Warburg, 1995; Northwestern U.P., 1995)

Amerika: The Man Who Disappeared, Franz Kafka (Penguin, 1995; New Directions, 2002)

The Land of Green Plums, Herta Müller (Granta, 1998)

Agnes, Peter Stamm (Bloomsbury, 1999)

The String of Pearls, Joseph Roth (Granta, 1999; US edition: *The Tale of the 1002nd Night*, St Martin's Press, 1998)

The Pollen Room, Zoë Jenny (Bloomsbury, 1999)

My Time with Antonioni, Wim Wenders (Faber, 2000)

Rebellion, Joseph Roth (Granta, 2000; Picador USA, 2000)

The Collected Shorter Fiction of Joseph Roth (Granta, 2001; US title, *The Collected Stories of Joseph Roth* (W. W. Norton, 2003))

The Wandering Jews, Joseph Roth (Granta, 2001; W. W. Norton, 2001)

On Film: Essays and Conversations, Wim Wenders (Faber, 2001)

The Snowflake Constant, Peter Stephan Jungk (Faber, 2002; US title, *Tigor*, Other Press, 2004))

The Hothouse, Wolfgang Koeppen (Granta, 2002; W. W. Norton, 2002)

Luck, Gert Hofmann (Harvill Press, 2002; New Directions, 2002)

A Sad Affair, Wolfgang Koeppen (Granta, 2003; W. W. Norton, 2003)

The Radetzky March, Joseph Roth (Granta, 2002)

What I Saw, Joseph Roth (Granta, 2003; W. W. Norton, 2004)

Report from a Parisian Paradise, Joseph Roth (Granta, 2003; W. W. Norton, 2004)

Storm of Steel, Ernst Jünger (Penguin, 2004)

Lichtenberg and the Little Flower Girl, Gert Hofmann (New
    Directions, 2004; CB editions, 2008)
The Perfect American, Peter Stephan Jungk (Other Press, 2004)
Party in the Blitz, Elias Canetti (Harvill, 2005; New Directions,
    2010)
The Stalin Front, Gert Ledig (NYRB, 2005)
An Innocent Soldier, Josef Holub (Arthur A. Levine, 2005)
In Strange Gardens and Other Stories, Peter Stamm (Other Press,
    2006)
Unformed Landscape, Peter Stamm (Other Press, 2006)
Child of All Nations, Irmgard Keun (Penguin, 2006)
The Zürau Aphorisms, Franz Kafka (Harvill Secker, 2006;
    Knopf, 2006)
Mother Courage and Her Children, Bertolt Brecht (Methuen, 2006)
Frost, Thomas Bernhard (Vintage, 2006)
The Seventh Well, Fred Wander (Granta, 2007; W. W. Norton,
    2007)
Metamorphosis and Other Stories, Franz Kafka (Penguin, 2007)
A Stranger to Myself, Willi Peter Reese (FSG, 2005)
Every Man Dies Alone, Hans Fallada (Melville House, 2009;
    UK title, *Alone In Berlin*, Penguin, 2009)
The Inheritance, Peter Stephan Jungk (Pushkin, 2010)
The Bars of Atlantis: Selected Essays, Durs Grünbein (with
    Crutchfield, Shields; FSG, 2010)
The Leviathan, Joseph Roth (New Directions, 2011)
Short Treatise on the Joys of Morphinism, Hans Fallada (Penguin,
    2011)
Seven Years, Peter Stamm (Other Press, 2011; Granta, 2012)
A Small Circus, Hans Fallada (Penguin, 2012)
We're Flying, Peter Stamm (Other Press, 2012; Granta, 2013)
My First Wife, Jakob Wassermann (Penguin, 2012)
The Emperor's Tomb, Joseph Roth (Granta, 2013; New
    Directions, 2013)
Youth, Wolfgang Koeppen (Dalkey Archive, 2013)

Selected Stories, Hans Fallada, (Penguin, 2013)
The Promised Land, Erich Maria Remarque (Vintage, 2014)
Berlin Alexanderplatz, Alfred Döblin (Penguin, 2014)

Introductions to

Flight Without End, Joseph Roth (Dent Everyman, 1984)
The Sheltering Sky, Paul Bowles (Penguin, 1999)
Payback, Gert Ledig (Granta, 2003)
Elected Friends: Robert Frost and Edward Thomas to One Another
(Other Press, 2004)
How German Is It?, Walter Abish (Penguin, 2005)

Contributed to

Another Round at The Pillars, ed. David Harsent (Cargo Press,
1999)
Strong Words: Modern Poets on Modern Poetry, ed. W. N. Herbert
and Matthew Hollis (Bloodaxe, 2000)
Arturo Di Stefano (with John Berger, Christopher Lloyd;
Merrell, 2001)

Poems in anthologies

Poetry Introduction 5 (Faber, 1982)
Some Contemporary Poets of Britain and Ireland, ed. Michael
Schmidt (Carcanet, 1983)
Emergency Kit: Poems for Strange Times, ed. Matthew Sweeney
and Jo Shapcott (Faber, 1996)
Extravagant Strangers: A Literature of Belonging, ed. Caryl Phillips
(Faber, 1997)
Penguin Modern Poets Vol. 13 (Penguin, 1998)
Here to Eternity, ed. Andrew Motion (Faber, 2001)
The 20th Century in Poetry, ed. Simon Rae and Michael
Hulse(Ebury Press, 2011)
London: A History in Verse, ed. Mark Ford (Harvard, 2012)

Interviews

In conversation with Stephen Knight (*Poetry Wales*, Summer
    1997, Issue 33.1)
In conversation with Fran Brearton (*Thumbscrew*, Spring/
    Summer 1999, No. 13)
Interview in *Talking with Poets* (ed. Harry Thomas, Other
    Press, 2004)
In conversation with Mark Thwaite (*Ready Steady Book*,
    October 2005)
In conversation with Rosanna Licari (*Stylus Poetry Journal*,
    March 2009)
In conversation with Jena Woodhouse (*Heat*, Summer 2009,
    No. 21)

Contributors

Eric Bliman holds an MFA from the University of Florida and a PhD from the University of Cincinnati. His poems have appeared in the *Times Literary Supplement*, *The Southern Review*, *Quarterly West*, *Subtropics*, and other journals. In 2012, his chapbook *Travel and Leisure* won the Poetry Society of America's Chapbook Fellowship. He recently joined the English faculty of Penn State at Harrisburg.

Charles Boyle is a lapsed poet – *The Age of Cardboard and String* (Faber, 2001) – and current writer of fiction: *24 for 3* (Bloomsbury, 2008) and *The Manet Girl* (Salt, 2013). He is founder-editor of CB editions.

James Buchan was for many years a correspondent of the *Financial Times* in the Middle East, and later in central Europe and the US. He has written more than a dozen works of fiction and history. His latest book is *Days of God: The Revolution in Iran and Its Consequences* (2012).

Fred D'Aguiar was born in London in 1960 of Guyanese parents and brought up in Guyana. He has published twelve books of poetry and fiction and a play as well as numerous essays. His fifth collection of poems, *Continental Shelf* (Carcanet, 2009) was a Poetry Book Society Choice and was shortlisted for the T. S. Eliot Prize. His latest collection is *The Rose of Toulouse* (2013). He teaches at Virginia Tech.

Curtis D'Costa received his BA from the University of St Thomas in Houston, TX, in 2006, and his MFA in Creative Writing from the University of Florida in 2008. He teaches literature and composition in Houston and serves on the advisory board of the Texas Nature Project.

Arturo Di Stefano was born in England of Italian parents in 1955. He studied Painting at Goldsmiths' College, London, the Royal College of

Art, London, and Accademia Albertina, Turin. His work is included in many public and private collections. He lives and works in London.

Andrew Elliott's poetry collections include *Lung Soup* (Blackstaff, 2009) and *Mortality Rate* (CB editions, 2013).

Hans Magnus Enzensberger was born in Kaufbeuren, Germany in 1929. He has written poetry, essays, as well as works for theatre, film, opera, radio drama. He was the founder of the quarterly *Kursbuch* in 1965 and a monthly, *TransAtlantik*, in 1980. From 1985 to 2005, Enzensberger ran an imprint of his own, the Frankfurt-based *Die Andere Bibliothek*, which released a classic masterpiece each month. Enzensberger's own work has been translated extensively into more than forty languages.

Mary Beth Ferda completed her MFA at the University of Florida in 2009. Her poems have appeared in the *Times Literary Supplement*, *Hayden's Ferry Review* and *FENCE*, among other publications. She works as a licensed massage therapist in Huntington, West Virginia.

Mark Ford is a Professor in the English Department at University College London. Recent publications include a volume of poetry, *Six Children* (2011), a collection of essays, *Mr and Mrs Stevens and Other Essays* (2011), a translation of Raymond Roussel's *Nouvelles Impressions d'Afrique* (2011), and an anthology of the poetry of London, *London: A History in Verse* (2012).

Durs Grünbein was born in Dresden in 1962 and lives in Berlin. He has published thirteen poetry collections, a diary, and three books of essays, as well as translations of Aeschylus, Seneca and Juvenal. His work has been awarded numerous major German and International prizes and his poetry has been translated into many languages. Recent publications in English include *Ashes for Breakfast: Selected Poems* (FSG, 2005), *The Bars of Atlantis: Selected Essays* (FSG, 2010), *Descartes' Devil: Three Meditations* (2010), *The Vocation of Poetry* (2011) and the forthcoming *Mortal Diamond* (2013), from Upper West Side Philosophers, Inc.

Tessa Hadley has written four novels, including *The Master Bedroom* and *The London Train*, and two collections of short stories. A new novel, *Clever Girl*, will be published in May 2013. She has also written one book of criticism, *Henry James and the Imagination of Pleasure*. She publishes stories regularly in *The New Yorker*, reviews for the *London Review of Books* and the *Guardian*, and teaches at Bath Spa University.

Saskia Hamilton is the author of *As for Dream* (2001), *Divide These* (2005) and *Corridor* (forthcoming, 2014), and is the editor of *The Letters of Robert Lowell* (2005) and co-editor of *Words in Air: The Complete Correspondence between Elizabeth Bishop and Robert Lowell* (2008). She teaches at Barnard College in New York City.

Alan Jenkins is the Deputy Editor of the *Times Literary Supplement*. He edited Ian Hamilton's *Collected Poems* (2013). Recent publications include *A Shorter Life* (2005) and *Drunken Boats* (2007), a new translation of Rimbaud's 'Le Bateau ivre'.

Lawrence Joseph is the author of five books of poetry, most recently *Into It* and *Codes, Precepts, Biases, and Taboos: Poems 1973–1993* (FSG); and two books of prose: *Lawyerland* (FSG) and *The Game Changed: Essays and Other Prose* (University of Michigan Press). He is presently Tinnelly Professor of Law at St John's University School of Law.

Rutger Kopland, the pseudonym of R. H. van den Hoofdakker (1934–2012), was one of the leading Dutch poets of his generation. He is the author of fifteen books of poetry, including his *Collected Poems* (2008), as well as several books of essays. Selections of his work in English have been translated by James Brockway, J. M. Coetzee, and others. His many awards include the 1988 P.C. Hooft-prize.

James Lasdun has written several books of fiction and poetry. He was born in London and now lives in the USA. His most recent books include *It's Beginning to Hurt* (stories) and *Water Sessions* (poetry).

William Logan is the author of eleven collections of poetry, most recently *Madame X* (Penguin, 2012), and five books of essays and reviews, most recently *Our Savage Art* (Columbia University Press, 2009). *The Undiscovered Country* received the National Book Critics Circle Award in criticism. He is the winner of the Randall Jarrell Award in Poetry Criticism.

Sarah Maguire is the Founder and Director of the Poetry Translation Centre. She has published four collections of poetry, most recently *The Pomegranates of Kandahar* (Chatto), shortlisted for the 2007 T. S. Eliot Prize. She is the only living English-language poet with a book in print in Malayalam.

Randall Mann is the author of two books of poems, *Breakfast with Thom Gunn* and *Complaint in the Garden*. A third collection, *Straight Razor*, is forthcoming from Persea Books. His poems and prose have appeared in the *Guardian*, *The New Republic*, *Paris Review*, *Poetry* and the *Washington Post*. He lives in San Francisco.

Jamie McKendrick has published six books of poetry, most recently *Out There* (2012). A selected poems, *Sky Nails*, was published by Faber in 2001. He edited *The Faber Book of 20th-Century Italian Poems* and has translated, among other things, Giorgio Bassani's *The Garden of the Finzi-Continis* and *The Gold-Rimmed Spectacles* as well as a volume of Valerio Magrelli's poems, *The Embrace*.

Andrew Motion is Professor of Creative Writing at Royal Holloway and co-founder of the online poetry collection, the Poetry Archive. He has received numerous awards for his poetry, and has published four celebrated biographies. His latest collection of poetry is *The Customs House* (2012).

André Naffis-Sahely is a poet and translates from the French and the Italian. His translations include Émile Zola's *Money*, Rashid Boudjedra's *The Barbary Figs* and Abdellatif Laâbi's *The Bottom of the Jar*. A selection of his poems is forthcoming in Oxford Poets 2013.

Dennis O'Driscoll's nine books of poetry include *New and Selected Poems* (Anvil Press, 2004), a Poetry Book Society Special Commendation, *Reality Check* (Anvil Press 2007; Copper Canyon Press, 2008) and *Dear Life* (Anvil Press, 2012; Copper Canyon Press, 2013). His forthcoming books are *The Outnumbered Poet: Critical and Autobiographical Essays* (Gallery Press) and, as editor, *A Michael Hamburger Reader* (Anvil Press).

Christopher Reid was Michael Hofmann's editor at Faber and Faber for most of the 1990s, in which role he was time and again made to feel redundant by Hofmann's immaculate copy. His own latest collection of poems, from Faber, is *Nonsense*.

Robin Robertson is from the north-east coast of Scotland. His fifth collection, *Hill of Doors*, was published in early 2013.

Stephen Romer is Maître de conférences at the University of Tours. He has published four collections of poetry; the latest, *Yellow Studio* (Oxford Poets, 2008) was shortlisted for the T. S. Eliot prize. He has also edited and translated two anthologies of French poetry, including Faber's *20th-Century French Poems* (2002), and most recently a version of Yves Bonnefoy's *The Arrière-pays* (Seagull, 2012). His *French Decadent Tales* is due from Oxford World's Classics in 2013.

Declan Ryan's poems and reviews have appeared in *Poetry Review, Poetry London, Night & Day* and elsewhere. He is working on a PhD on 'Perfect Speech' in the poems of Ian Hamilton and Lachlan Mackinnon and co-edits the *Days of Roses* anthology series.

Ralph Savarese is the author of *Reasonable People: A Memoir of Autism and Adoption*, and has published poems, essays, translations, opinion pieces and scholarship. He teaches at Grinnell College in Iowa.

Michael Schmidt is Writer in Residence at St John's College, Cambridge. He is a founder (1969), editorial and managing director of Carcanet Press, and a founder (1972) and general editor of *PN Review*. An anthologist, translator, critic and literary historian.

Frederick Seidel's many books of poems include *The Cosmos Trilogy, Ooga-Booga* and *Poems 1959–2009*. His newest collection, *Nice Weather*, was published in September 2012.

Andrew Shields lives in Basel, Switzerland. His many translations from the German include work by Hannah Arendt, Dieter M. Gräf, Durs Grünbein and Martin Heidegger.

Julian Stannard's latest collection is *The Parrots of Villa Gruber Discover Lapis Lazuli* (Salmon, 2011); this completes a trilogy of works concerning the city of Genoa. He is the author of *Fleur Adcock in Context: From Movement to Martians* (Edwin Mellen, 1997) and *The Poetic Achievements of Donald Davie and Charles Tomlinson* (Edwin Mellen, 2010). A study of Basil Bunting will be published by Northcote House in 2013. He is a Reader in English and Creative Writing at the University of Winchester.

George Szirtes's most recent books are *New and Collected Poems* (2008), *The Burning of the Books* (2009) and *Bad Machine* (2013). He also translates poetry and fiction from the Hungarian. Together with Helen Ivory he has recently co-edited *In Their Own Words* (2012), an anthology of contemporary poets writing about their practice.

Meg Tyler is a poet and Associate Professor of Humanities at Boston University, where she also directs the Poetry Reading Series. In 2012 she was the Fulbright Visiting Professor of Humanities and Social Sciences at the University of Innsbruck. 'Contemporary Poets and the Sonnet: a Trialogue (Paul Muldoon, Jeff Hilson and Meg Tyler)' recently appeared in *The Cambridge Companion to the Sonnet*, edited by A. D. Cousins and Peter Howarth.

Rosanna Warren is the Hanna Holborn Gray Distinguished Service Professor in the Committee on Social Thought at the University of Chicago. Her book of criticism, *Fables of the Self: Studies in Lyric Poetry*, came out in 2008. Her most recent books of poems are *Departure* (2003) and *Ghost in a Red Hat* (2011). She has received awards from the Academy of American Poets and the American Academy of Arts & Letters. She was a Chancellor of the Academy of American Poets from 1999 to 2005.

David Wheatley is the author of five books of poetry, most recently *Flowering Skullcap* (Wurm Press, 2012). He teaches at the University of Aberdeen.

Shaun Whiteside is a translator from German, French, Italian and Dutch. His first published translation, with Michael Hofmann, was Wim Wenders's *Emotion Pictures* (Faber, 1989)

C. K. Williams has won the Pulitzer Prize, the National Book Award and the National Book Critics Circle Award, among other honours. His latest books are *Writers Writing Dying*, a book of poems, and *In Time: Poets, Poems, and the Rest*, a book of essays. He is a member of the American Academy of Arts and Letters, and teaches in the Creative Writing Program at Princeton University.

Hugo Williams was born in 1942. He writes the 'Freelance' column in the *Times Literary Supplement* and lives in London. His latest collection is *West End Final* (2009).

Tony Williams's poetry has been shortlisted for the Aldeburgh, Portico and Michael Murphy Memorial Prizes, and was a Poetry Book Society Pamphlet Choice in 2011. *All the Bananas I've Never Eaten*, a collection of very short stories, was published by Salt in 2012. He teaches creative writing at Northumbria University.

Suzanne Zweizig's poetry has appeared in *32 Poems*, *The Beloit Poetry Journal*, *Poet Lore*, *Subtropics*, *Verse Daily*, *Waccamaw Review* and others. She has received fellowships from the MacDowell Colony, the Washington DC Arts Commission and the Virginia Center for the Creative Arts and, was a semi-finalist for The Nation/Discovery prize in 2003.

Acknowledgements

The editors are grateful to Alexandra Parsons, who visited Arturo Di Stefano's studio in East London to photograph his portrait of Hofmann, reproduced inside the book, as well as its counterproof, which graces the cover; and to Declan Ryan for help with editing and proofreading.

Rutger Kopland's 'Mens en schaap' is from *Geduldig gereedschap* (Amsterdam: Oorschot, 1993)

André Naffis-Sahely's 'Wunderkind' was originally published in *Poetry London*, Spring 2011.

Robin Robertson's 'The Translator' was first published in *A Painted Field* (1997) and is reprinted here courtesy of Picador.

Julian Stannard's 'Nothing Dreamier than Barracks!' is a revised version of an article that first appeared in *PN Review* 143, Volume 28 Number 3, January–February 2002.

Hugo Williams's 'King-Wilkinson' is included in *West End Final* (Faber, 2009).

ⒷB editions

Founded in 2007, CB editions publishes chiefly short
fiction (including work by Gabriel Josipovici, David
Markson and Dai Vaughan) and poetry (Fergus
Allen, Andrew Elliott, Beverley Bie Brahic, Nancy
Gaffield, J. O. Morgan, D. Nurkse). Writers published
in translation include Apollinaire, Andrzej Bursa,
Joaquín Giannuzzi, Gert Hofmann and Francis Ponge.

Books can be ordered from www.cbeditions.com.